COOKING
HUNAN-STYLE

COOKING HUNAN-STYLE

Louise Stallard

DRAKE PUBLISHERS INC.
NEW YORK

Published in 1973 by
Drake Publishers Inc.
381 Park Avenue South
New York, N.Y. 10016

Library of Congress Catalog Card Number 72-10489
ISBN 0-87749-423-1

Printed in Italy

Prepared and produced for the publisher by BMG Productions, Incorporated

Photographs by Meryl Joseph

For Maria, Peter, Scot and Tracy, Annie and Teddy, Scottie, Lorian, Frankie and Anna, Christopher and Amanda, Jean and Eddie, John and Margaret, Courtney and Patrick, Sally, Nelson, Trevor, Susan and Betsy, Eden, Matt and JoAlice

CONTENTS

ACKNOWLEDGEMENTS

The author wishes to thank Harry Shum, former manager, and the Hunam Restaurant for their assistance in the preparation of photographs for this book. Thanks also to Rhona Bross and to Joyce Garrick and to Pao Peter Lee and the staff of the Flower Drum Restaurant for their help and encouragement.

COOKING
HUNAN-STYLE

BEFORE
YOU
BEGIN

A new kind of Chinese food has been winning devoted fans in the West: It is the food of the "western provinces" of Hunan, Szechuan, and Kweichow. If China were the same shape as the United States, which it isn't, and if the provinces bore the same relation to their country's outline as the states do to the U.S., which they do not, we might think of Hunan, Szechuan, and Kweichow as being in about the same positions as Arkansas, Missouri, and Alabama. Just as Kentucky was the "Far West" in colonial times, so were Hunan, Szechuan, and Kweichow west of the capitals of China. That they seem south-central on the map today is neither here nor there!

These inland provinces had a particular handicap that they overcame brilliantly in developing a singular cuisine: There was very little salt imported so far over the mountains, and that little did not reach people of modest means. Hot peppers and other spices were used instead of salt, and an accommodation of necessity brought about a glorious new cuisine.

Most people in the United States think of Cantonese food as "Chinese" food, but the food of the western provinces has always been popular in China and other countries of Asia. Hunanese restaurants prospered years ago in Peking and other cities. Whereas Cantonese cuisine relies heavily on seafoods and vegetables, Hunan dishes feature a great deal of meat, particularly pork. Very little thickening is used in sauces (as opposed to the Cantonese practice of thickening with cornstarch), and instead of being somewhat bland, very hot chilis enliven Hunan food. MSG is not much used since there is no need to bring up the taste of spices that are pretty stout by themselves! Hunan meals are much heartier than Cantonese meals; vegetables are important, but meat is the serious nourishment.

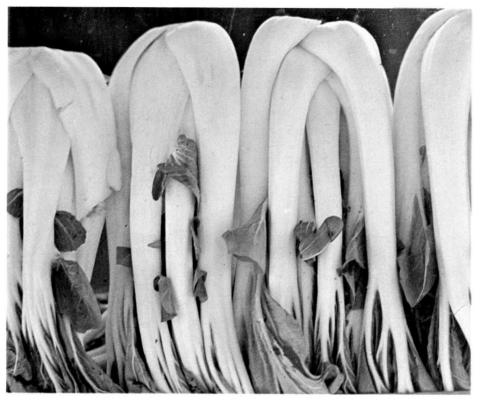

Bok choy

One of the great additions to the world of food is the Hunan *pot*. More than a soup, yet not like a stew, this slow-cooked one-dish meal can be made by many recipes. It is always delicious, however, and beautiful besides. It should also be very popular with hostesses in the West who have to feed uncertain numbers of people at times not absolutely set (such as a crowd returning from a football game). Another Hunan contribution is dry-marinated pork. Salt and hot peppers preserved meat before the days of refrigeration. It is our good luck that such a delicious discovery was made.

Until modern times there was no seafood available in Hunan, but the taste of saltwater fish was popular, so an imitation was developed, fish-taste marinade. Freshwater fish were plentiful, however, and some of the most delicious ways of preparing them come to us from Hunan.

Many vegetables are used in Hunan dishes, especially root and leafy green vegetables. The root vegetables are important in pots and soups and are also eaten alone. Some of the most sophisticated vegetable cookery in the world is to be found in Hunan. Melons are popular both as vegetables (such as bitter winter melons) and as fruits (cantaloupes).

Hot chilis are very important to Hunan cooking. What to call the different varieties is a vexed question; the Chinese name is usually a Cantonese corruption of a word from another Chinese dialect, and that rendered into uncertain Roman letters and more uncertain English pronounciation. In this book the Latin American (mostly Mexican) names have been used since they seem to be in more general (and uniform) use. The fresh chilis you may need include the following.

Serranos: small, dark green, pointed, *very* hot chilis. Available fresh and canned. (Be sure to get those canned in brine only; the pickled ones will give the dishes a very strange flavor.)

Jalapeños: usually a little larger, lighter, and with blunter ends than serranos. Very hot.

Italian peppers: long, thin green or red hot peppers. Widely available.

Chilis poblanos: rather like green bell peppers but darker in color. Usually poblanos are mild, but they can be hot. Taste before using.

Fresh chilis are sometimes available in vegetable and specialty stores and often in stores serving the Latin American community. If you do not find them locally, ask a store to order them for you.

Several dried hot peppers are important in Hunan cooking. They include *Szechuan pepper,* also known as *fagara.* It comes in reddish peppercorns a little smaller than black pepper. Its flavor is rather mild and spicy, somewhat like stick cinnamon but sharper. Szechuan pepper is also available ground in some Oriental grocery stores, but unless you plan to use it up at once, buy peppercorns; they will keep their flavor much longer than the ground pepper. Usually, Szechuan pepper can be crushed sufficiently for use with a mortar and pestle. If the pepper is to go into a smooth sauce, sift it through a fine sieve after crushing.

Chilis pasillas are long black dried peppers. They are rigid when dry but will soften in a few minutes in hot water. Almost all recipes specify that the seeds be removed from chilis pasillas; they are very, very hot. They will be easy to remove when the chili has softened.

Chilis Japonesas are light red and look like small Italian peppers, but they are not especially hot. Their taste is interesting, though.

Chilis pequines are tiny *very* hot red peppers. They are measured not by the spoonful but by the pepper. Count carefully! It is interesting to note that chilis pequines were being called that—chilis of Peking—at the time of the Spanish conquest of Mexico. So much for the Western Hemisphere's being primitive and isolated and knowing nothing of the rest of the world!

Cayenne—ground red pepper—is used in dry-marinating pork. It can also be used to create a hot taste when other chilis are not available. Buy the smallest can of cayenne you can find and use it up fast; it loses a lot of its punch if it is kept on the shelf long. Try keeping it in the refrigerator.

Fresh chilis spoil quickly, so buy them in small quantities. You may freeze them by blanching them quickly in boiling water, drying them, and freezing at once. Canned chilis keep indefinitely, and dried chilis will be fine if they are kept in a dry place (to prevent mold); a canister with a loose lid in a fairly warm place would be ideal.

Dry mustard is not exactly a pepper, but it is an important ingredient in many Hunan recipes. Again, buy it in the smallest container available and keep it in the refrigerator after it is opened.

Other ingredients with which you may not be familiar are *fresh ginger root* and *fresh coriander*. Ginger is available in Chinese grocery stores and sometimes at specialty shops. (It looks like long knobby new potatoes.) It is seasonal and perishable (dries out at room temperature and develops mold in the refrigerator—the mold is harmless and doesn't affect the taste; scrape it off), but it freezes well. Just wrap air tight in foil and freeze before washing or peeling. Cut off as much as is needed from the frozen root when cooking. Fresh coriander looks like broad-leaf parsley but has an entirely different taste that is hard to describe. Coriander is not hot but has a subtle taste unlike anything else. A man I know who does not like it says it tastes soapy. Well, yes and no. Try it for yourself and see if you like it. It is sometimes available in vegetable stores and usually in Chinese or Latin American groceries. Dried coriander leaves, not as good as fresh but better than no coriander at all, are available by mail order. (See Sources of Supplies.) Coriander also grows wild in many parts of the United States and other temperate countries. Riverside Park in New York raises an enormous supply. Scout your local fields; your coriander shortage may be over! Fresh coriander can be frozen. Clean and store in small plastic bags and freeze quickly. Fresh coriander comes with the roots on the sprigs. If you are going to keep it in the refrigerator a few days without freezing, leave the roots on and do not wash it. Store in a paper bag instead of a plastic one. If there is too much moisture around coriander, it will turn into a most unpleasant swamp in record time.

Dried mushrooms, dried shrimp, and dried lily flowers are all available in Oriental groceries. Since they are so light and stable, they are easy to obtain by mail order, and they keep very well. Chinese rice wine is sometimes hard to find, but Japanese sake will do as a substitute. Soy sauce is now available in every supermarket. The recipes in this book were developed with Kikkoman-brand Japanese soy sauce, a personal preference. Kikkoman is thinner, less sweet, and saltier than Chinese brands tasted. A taste for seasonings just before serving, a good idea, anyway, will allow you to adjust salt if the soy sauce you are using is different from Kikkoman.

EQUIPMENT

You do not need unusual kitchen equipment to cook Hunan food. You probably have everything you need already.

First you should have a dependable, controllable heat source. A gas flame is best, but the new fast electric elements may work for you if you are accustomed to them. Some very delicate dishes require very closely regulated heat; an alcohol or butane flame would be a good investment if you usually cook with electricity.

A good minute minder and a clock with a sweep second hand are great aids in cooking Hunan properly.

Since so many ingredients in Hunan recipes need to be sliced, shredded, or minced, you will need good knives and a good cutting board. Your knives should be the best quality you can afford; never use them on hard surfaces and never let them soak in water. Have them sharpened professionally as often as necessary. Use a hand stone to keep edges keen between overhauls. One large and one small knife are needed. Add to them later.

Chinese chefs and experienced cooks use 1-pound cleavers for cutting and chopping. A cleaver (or two used in tandem) in the hands of an experienced cook is a very efficient tool, but unfortunately it can do a lot of damage while the cook is getting experi-

Basic Chinese cooking equipment: a 14" wok, cleaver, large and small knives, ladle, broad spatula, and strainer (very handy for retrieving food). The brush is a wok scrubber.

enced. If you are learning to use a cleaver, take care and go slowly. Remember to use it in moderation; if you hack up the surface of the cutting board severely, splinters will work out and mingle with the food you are chopping, giving an unpleasant taste and texture. Remember, too, that if you hack heavy bones, chips are going to fly. Wear safety glasses.

A compromise (safer) method of cutting that allows processes usually reserved to the cleaver, such as hacking a whole chicken or duck, is heavy-knife-and-mallet. Place the cutting edge of the knife exactly where the cut is to be made, then hit it on the back with the mallet. This method will cut almost anything the cleaver will. Do not use one of your fine knives; a sturdy butcher knife works well.

The traditional cooking pan for stir frying is the *wok*. Shaped like an inverted coolie hat, a wok provides several cooking surfaces in one vessel. Oil collects in the bottom, and food may be fried in it or pushed up the shallow sides to drain and cook at a lower temperature. In Chinese restaurants you will see ranks of enormous woks lined up over the heat source and beneath faucets plumbed so that the woks can be used, emptied, washed out, and used again without any lost motion, an arrangement the home cook might envy.

If you buy a wok, select one that is quite heavy for its size; it should have a lid. A large wok is much more practical than a small one. Look for one at least 12" across; even larger would be better. Make sure you get the ring or stand to hold the wok over the heat source.

A wok is very nice to have, but you can also use a large heavy skillet very successfully. Most of the recipes in this book were tested in an old black iron skillet, and it worked very well. The skillet should also have a lid.

A very large deep pot with a lid is needed for making stock, and it can become a steamer with the addition of a rack. A very large pot handsome enough to go to the table is necessary for cooking and serving pots. Earthenware is lighter; porcelain-clad iron is very durable and good-looking, though it tends to be very heavy, especially when full of hot soup.

A blender is the most efficient way to blend ginger and garlic and other ingredients for sauce. It is almost an essential. A food mill that will grind meat is useful but is not as much used as a blender. A garlic press is nice to have, as is a European-style rolling pin (long, thin, no handles).

Serving platters and bowls are not cooking equipment, but an attractive selection of these dishes can make quite a lot of difference in the way your meal looks and is received. Take inventory and plan to get some dark, some light-colored, some ornate, and some plain serving dishes in a variety of shapes.

You will also want to get some small and some large soup bowls. These bowls (the smaller ones for clear soups and those served between the courses as taste breaks; the larger ones for important main-dish soups) should be fairly deep as opposed, say, to cream soup plates. In China there would not be saucers under the bowls, but you may want to use them.

China soup spoons are a thoughtful and attractive addition to your table; they are available in Oriental stores and may be very simple and inexpensive or very expensive indeed. Besides looking pretty, they are very good for eating hot soup since the porcelain does not conduct heat from the bowl to the handle as do metal spoons. The broad shallow bowl helps cool each bite of soup as you are about to eat it. You will probably find that you use your porcelain soup spoons for many other purposes as well: They are just right for sauce and jelly spoons.

Chopsticks are the best implements for eating Hunan food. Elegance in chopsticks is a brand-new set of wooden ones for each guest; avoid the silver and ivory ones or anything fancy. Of course, chopsticks can be washed and used again; they are very good for stir frying foods and adding ingredients to the cooking pan. Needless to say, if anyone at your table is uncomfortable with chopsticks, provide forks. It is unfair to ask guests to learn a new skill in public (and without any warning).

COOKING METHODS

Most of the recipes in this book have one factor in common; they are *fast*. Please always read the recipe through before planning to cook it or beginning its preparation. That way you can avoid the plight of the woman who had three couples ready to eat when she went to bring her very ambitious dinner to a finish. Imagine her distress when the next paragraph in the elaborate recipe said, "Store in a cool dark place for 36 hours."

Many main-dish recipes are cooked by stir frying, cooking the thinly sliced or chopped ingredients in very hot oil for a very short time. This technique is not difficult if you follow some simple precautions. *All ingredients must be prepared and ready before you begin to cook.* It is impossible to emphasize this requirement too strongly. The cooking process goes so fast that once the cooking has begun, there is no time to cut or prepare ingredients to be added later.

If you need more of any dish, cook it in two batches instead of doubling the recipe. A crowded skillet will not cook properly.

Since the ingredients must be prepared ahead, anyway, stir frying lends itself to what I think of as public-appearance cooking. The cut vegetables and meats will look very attractive around your chafing dish, and you will look very glamorous and efficient whipping up a dish before the guests' eyes.

Light vegetable oil, such as peanut oil, safflower oil, or top-quality lard, is used for stir frying. Some dishes taste better with one or the other, and those recipes say so. Good lard is packed by the major meat-packing houses and should be available at your supermarket. If you have a local slaughterhouse that handles pigs, it may have fresh lard; if so, do try it. Ask for leaf lard, the most delicate kind; it makes very good pastry as well. Whatever shortening you choose, it should be very fresh, of course. It should be very hot, but not burning, when other ingredients are added. If it burns in the skillet, throw it out, wash the pan, and start over. Add oil sparingly at the beginning of the cooking process; you can add a bit more later if necessary. Except for a few vegetable dishes, you should not have any oil to pour off at the end of the cooking process. Keep in mind that all the oil you put in the pan is going to be *eaten*.

Just as you need to have all the ingredients ready before you begin to cook, it is also a good idea to have your diners on hand. If you have to serve a dinner at an uncertain time, consider one of the hearty soups or pots or do the cooking itself after the crowd is actually in view. A few dishes really can't be held, and their recipes so note.

Chinese cabbage

MEALS AND MENUS

The traditional Chinese pattern of eating includes an early breakfast (very unlike ours) and two other meals of equal size and importance. For eight people one of these important meals might consist of six or eight main dishes plus a soup and rice but rarely a dessert. The main dishes would include meat dishes, fish dishes, and vegetable dishes. More elaborate meals for special occasions and for formal entertaining would have many more courses.

A meal for people used to eating Western style should be considerably less elaborate. I have found that a good rule of thumb on amount is one stir-fry-type dish (those calling for ½ pound of meat) for each 1½ diners, with any awkward arithmetic resolved in the direction of your guests' appetites. Four hearty eaters would get three dishes; four ladies watching their weights would get two. The stir-fry recipes in this book make one dish of the kind we are discussing.

Soup is not usually served as a first course in China but is eaten instead throughout the meal and between other courses. If you serve soup first, make sure it doesn't kill the appetite for and the taste of the foods to follow. If you serve it throughout the meal, the soup should be in contrast to the other dishes: light and delicate to break a series of spicy dishes, spicy to enliven bland ones.

In planning a menu overall, there are two important factors to consider. The first is who will be eating. What are their tastes? Will they take to new dishes? Do they like hot spicy foods? The best meal in the world will not be successful if these questions are not considered. You can certainly serve some adventurous dishes but make sure there is something everyone can enjoy.

The second consideration is *contrast*. A meal made up entirely of hot spicy dishes would be like an aria of unrelieved high Cs: nobody could stand it. In fact, three hot dishes are probably the practical limit even in elaborate meals, and those three should be varied. More than three hot dishes get to tasting alike, just as too many perfumes sampled at once lose their scent. Keep in mind that the amounts of spices are suggestions, not rigid requirements. With the recipes available, it is not difficult to choose dishes that contrast in color, dominant flavor, texture, and even temperature. Consider also the colors in each dish; an interesting combination will make the food *seem* to taste better. If your meal is to be served in courses, make sure there is contrast between them, too.

The presentation of food is important to its enjoyment, a factor too often overlooked in Western dining. Give careful consideration to the way your Chinese dishes are served. Serve each recipe on a background that makes it look best.

Tea is the beverage we usually associate with Chinese food, but Hunan food takes very well to cold beer or chilled, not-too-dry white wine. In China soup would be drunk with the main dish, and tea would not be served throughout the meal but would be brought with rice as a last light course. Please don't drown your dinner in tea. By the way, it is said that Chinese teacups have no handles because "too hot for hands, too hot for mouth." Not only will excessively hot tea burn your mouth (and not be good for your stomach), it will also drown the taste of your food. Serve it if you like, but sparingly.

Mixing Hunan dishes and Western dishes at the same meal is perfectly all right. Some very successful menus combine the things you like best from both cuisines. Do not be bound by rigid rules. Note also that some of the recipes in this book (see Index) make elegant and unusual first courses or hors d'oeuvres at a Western-style meal or party, though they are not traditionally served that way in China.

Dessert is usually not eaten after meals in China but rather as between-meal snacks. You can certainly serve it if you want to, however. Just keep it in harmony with the rest of the meal. (Remember those high Cs!)

INSCRUTABLE ETIQUETTE

If you are fortunate enough to be invited to dinner with Chinese friends, you may find a few words about etiquette helpful. Though we tend to think of people from the Orient as shy and reserved, your expressed admiration and appreciation of the occasion and surroundings will be very much in order, as will your respectful attention to older people present.

Usually, all the main dishes for a meal are put on the table at once. Help yourself to those near you and offer to serve the plates of those who cannot reach the dishes you can. Use their chopsticks if no serving spoon is provided. They are not supposed to touch the mouth when you eat, so they are quite sanitary.

It is perfectly good form to lift your rice bowl from the table and hold it close to your mouth when eating from it. Indeed, it is almost impossible to eat rice with chopsticks without getting into range! Also, it is all right to take rather noisy sips of soup; mixing air with the soup not only cools it but is supposed to develop its flavor. You don't have to slurp your soup if it doesn't come naturally to you, but you may not glare at those who do.

You probably wouldn't, anyway, but DO NOT blow your nose noisily in company; it is considered an intensely private function, which it certainly is.

In the West you will probably find a napkin at your place. If there isn't a napkin, you will no doubt be given hot damp towels after any messy courses. If you think of it, a tissue in the pocket might be handy just as a fail safe.

A note expressing your pleasure in the dinner extended to you is always in good taste, as are flowers for your hostess. Send them, however; no lady, East or West, can cope with getting flowers into water, greeting guests, and serving a meal all at the same time!

LOUISE STALLARD
New York, 1973

POULTRY

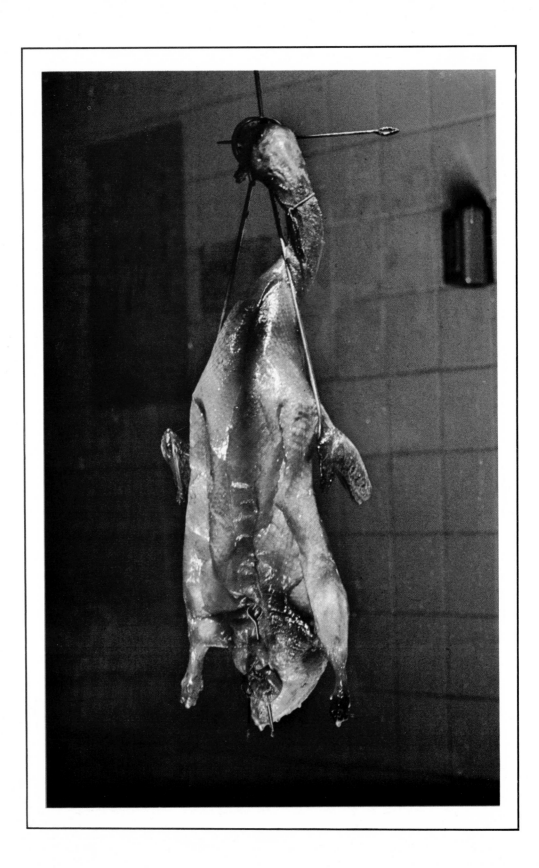

POULTRY

Chicken is a mainstay in Hunan cooking. Soups, first courses, main dishes, and pastries all feature it. (It is possible that the popularity of poultry in China before the days of fast transportation and good refrigeration owed something to the fact that it could always be kept fresh—alive—until ready to use!) Chicken is second only to pork as the "favorite" meat. Duck is also used more in China than it is in the West, and many festive dishes feature it.

We are fortunate that in recent years both the supply and quality of chicken available here have gone up. Tender chicken is not hard to find; in fact, if anything is in short supply, it seems to be stewing hens. See if your butcher can get them for you; they do make better soup and stock.

Duck is available all year frozen. To use in these recipes, thaw completely according to package directions, wash and dry, and proceed as with freshly killed duck. The variety of chicken and duck dishes is endless. The recipes in the following section are really only intended to whet your imagination. Just be sure not to overcook the delicate chicken meat in recipes in which it is the main ingredient.

Cold chicken dishes taste better if the meat and sauce are not served icy but at cool room temperature. If you have stored the components of cold dishes in the refrigerator, take them out half an hour or so before serving so that they can moderate a bit.

Several of the dishes following make excellent hors d'oeuvres; check the recipes.

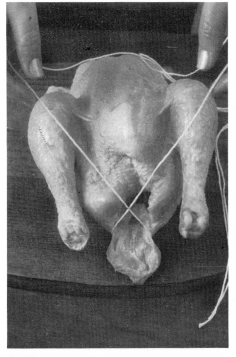

a

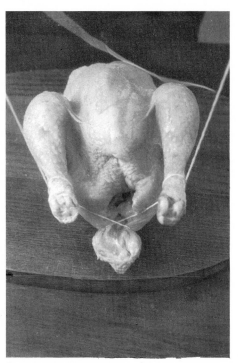

b

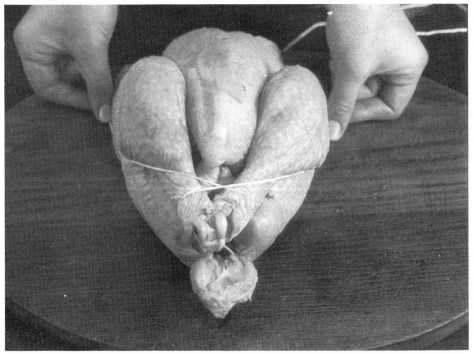

c

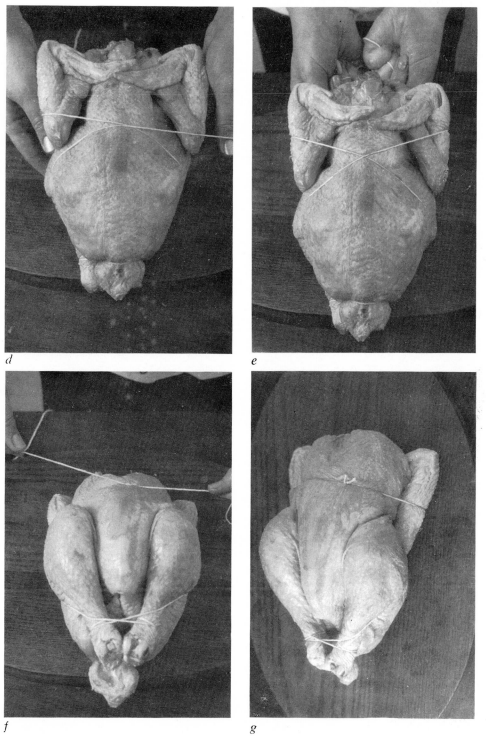

a) Place center of 4' string under the bird's tail and cross. b) Take string outside legs and wrap toward center. c) Cross string and draw around middle of legs toward chicken's back. d) Turn bird on its breast. Cross strings at mid-back. e) Take string around the wings (tips tucked behind). f) Tie strings tight over the breast. g) Cut off any excess string. The bird is ready to cook.

Chinese Roast Chicken (first step)

CHICKEN IN A POT

1 stewing fowl, about 7 pounds (or 2 frying chickens)
  water barely to cover
¾ cup soy sauce
¼ cup sweet sherry
1 piece fresh ginger about 1″ × ½″, sliced
1 clove garlic, peeled and crushed
2 teaspoons sugar
1 large or 2 medium onions, roughly chopped

Wash the bird inside and out and dry thoroughly with paper towels. Pull some of the fat from the inside of the chicken and render it over medium heat in a skillet large enough to hold the trussed chicken. Brown the bird on all sides, taking care not to let it cook too much—medium heat and patience work best here.

Place the browned chicken in a heavy pot and add water barely to cover. Bring to a rolling boil, then reduce heat so broth simmers. Add the other ingredients and cover the pot tightly. Cook gently until the chicken is tender when tested with a fork but not falling off the bones.

To serve, remove the chicken from the stock and let it cool. Cut it into bite-sized pieces and serve with reheated and reduced pot liquor.

If there is a lot of soup left, it can be used as sauce for other dishes or served suitably diluted with sliced dried mushrooms cooked in it. Very good.

WHITE CUT CHICKEN
(Basic Stewed Chicken)

1 fowl, about 7 pounds (The older chicken will make a tastier dish.)
7 cups water

You will need a large heavy pot with a tight lid to make this dish. It should not be too deep—you will want to retrieve the bird easily; a Dutch oven would be good.

Wash the chicken inside and out and put in the pot in *cold* water. Over high heat bring the pot to a rolling boil. Put on the cover and at once reduce the heat so that the pot simmers. Check the chicken for tenderness after 1½ hours and every half hour thereafter. It should be tender but not coming apart. When it is done, remove the chicken from the broth and let it cool. Store it well wrapped in the refrigerator. Save the broth for cooking or to use as a delicious soup base.

White cut chicken can be eaten as it is, cut into small chunks, bones and all, and served with soy sauce. Meat from the chicken can also be used in all recipes that call for cooked chicken.

QUICK POACHED CHICKEN

1 frying chicken, about 3 pounds
6 cups water

Put the water into a heavy pot with a tight-fitting lid and bring
it to a boil. Meanwhile, wash the chicken. When water is boiling,
put the chicken into the pot. Cover immediately and reduce heat
so that the broth simmers. Check for tenderness after 15 minutes
and very frequently thereafter; the bird should be done in a very
short time. (It will cook even quicker if it is allowed to warm up
from the refrigerator before cooking.)

Poached frying chicken can be used for any recipes calling for
cooked chicken, and it is especially delicate in dishes with light,
subtle sauces.

The broth is good for cooking and is easy to clarify; it makes
an elegant base for your most ambitious soups.

CHICKEN VELVET

  2 whole raw breasts from frying chickens
  3 tablespoons water
1 ½ teaspoons cornstarch
  3 egg whites
  1 teaspoon salt
 ¼ teaspoon white pepper
 ½ cup unsalted chicken broth
  1 tablespoon soy sauce
  1 tablespoon sweet sherry
 ½ cup finely sliced ham or cured roast pork

Skin and bone chicken breasts and cut them into very fine shreds. A cleaver (or two cleavers) and a good chopping block are the fastest implements, but a sharp knife used to slice, then mince, then chop, will do. Sprinkle the chicken with a little water from the 3 tablespoons if it seems to dry out while you are cutting it.

When chicken is finely cut, mix the rest of the water, the cornstarch, egg whites, salt, and pepper and stir into the chicken. Heat a skillet over medium heat and grease it with a teaspoon of oil. Pour in enough of the chicken mixture to barely cover the bottom of the pan and cook gently, stirring and pushing with a' spatula. When the chicken is just white, remove the batch from the pan and repeat cooking procedure. Use only enough oil to keep the chicken from sticking. Keep the already cooked batches on a warmed platter and serve as soon as all the chicken and the sauce are ready.

To make the sauce, combine chicken broth, soy sauce, and sherry. Bring to a boil and let reduce slightly. Stir in the ham or pork and pour over the chicken velvet.

This dish can be made also by beating two of the egg whites as for a soufflé and adding them to the chicken mixture. Then teaspoonfuls of the mixture are dropped into deep fat and cooked only until they are very pale brown. Whichever method is used, the chicken should be only just done and never overcooked.

Another delicious variation is adding ½ cup finely sliced and chopped white mushrooms to the chicken mixture before cooking. Canned mushrooms may be substituted, but fresh ones are better.

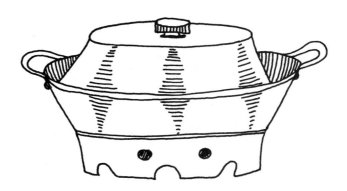

CHINESE ROAST CHICKEN

1 5-pound chicken (A capon would be excellent.)
 water to half cover chicken
1 cup soy sauce
2 tablespoons sugar
2 tablespoons sherry
1 piece fresh ginger about 1″ × ½″, minced
1 medium onion, diced

Wash chicken and truss it so it will hold its shape while cooking. Place the chicken in a heavy pan and add just enough water to come to its wings. Remove chicken and add the rest of the ingredients to the pot and bring to a boil. Return chicken to the pot and boil 15 minutes. Remove from heat and let stand at least 30 minutes.

Heat the oven to 500° F. Remove the chicken from cooking stock and dry thoroughly. Rub with just enough oil to moisten the breast and legs. Place the bird on a rack over a roasting pan and cook until completely browned, about 10 or 15 minutes. Allow bird to stand outside the oven 15 or 20 minutes to reabsorb juices if it is to be carved. Serve cooking stock, strained, separately, or thicken it with cornstarch to make gravy. Taste for seasonings.

CHICKEN WITH VEGETABLES

2 whole raw breasts of chicken
6 whole heads of broccoli
12 tiny white carrots (these will be canned, probably) or 12 tiny Belgian carrots
2 tablespoons oil
2 teaspoons cornstarch
1 teaspoon salt
½ teaspoon white pepper
¼ cup unsalted chicken broth or water

Skin and bone chicken breasts and cut meat into ½" cubes. Wash and dry broccoli (let drain for several hours) and cut each head into flowerets about ½" in diameter. (Use the stems for soup or another recipe, say Chicken Livers and Gizzards with Vegetables.) Drain the carrots and dry them with paper towels. If tiny carrots are not available, a good substitute would be sweet (nonhot) white radishes or celery heart.

When ready to cook and serve, heat the oil in a skillet. Keep heat medium. Sauté without browning the chicken on both sides. It should just turn opaque white. When you turn the chicken, add the broccoli flowerets to the skillet, stirring to coat them with oil. Reduce heat as much as possible, cover the pan, and cook for 3 minutes. Test the broccoli; it should be crisp-tender and still bright green. Mix the rest of the ingredients and pour into the pan. Increase heat slightly and cook, stirring carefully, just until sauce is thickened and coats chicken and broccoli. Very carefully stir in carrots and just heat through.

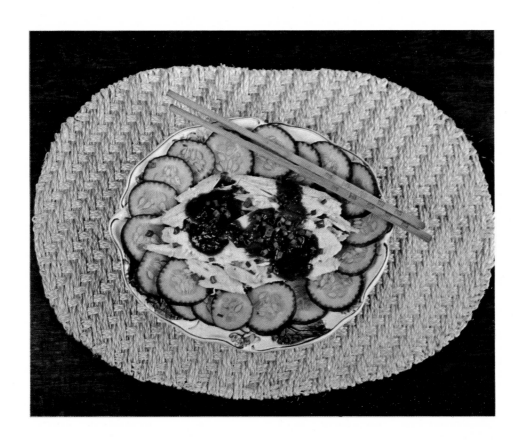

COLD CHICKEN WITH FRESH GINGER AND GARLIC SAUCE

    breast and thighs from one chicken (a fryer about 3 pounds) or a similar
    amount of leftover cooked chicken
¾ cups unsalted chicken stock or water
 2 tablespoons soy sauce
¼ teaspoon dry mustard
½ teaspoon sugar
    fresh ginger to taste
 2 or more cloves of garlic, peeled
 2 cucumbers, sliced
 1 whole scallion or sprigs of fresh chives

Both the chicken and the sauce for this dish need to be cooked, then thoroughly cooled, so start preparations early on the day it is to be served or, better yet, the day before.

Poach the chicken in about 3 cups unsalted water. Do not overcook; it should be tender but not falling off the bones. Let it cool completely in the stock. If it is to be kept more than the time it takes to cool, store in the refrigerator.

To make the sauce, take enough stock from the chicken pot to give ¾ cup after all the fat is skimmed off. (Or use water; canned stock or broth made from bouillon cubes is too salty and combined with the soy sauce will make a briny sauce.) In a blender combine the stock, soy sauce, mustard, sugar, ginger,* and garlic. Blend until the mixture is smooth. If you do not have a blender, cut up the garlic and ginger and pound in a mortar with a pestle until smooth and add to liquids.

Pour into a saucepan and bring to a boil. Reduce heat so that the sauce simmers and cook uncovered until it is about the consistency of thin hollandaise. This will take some little time if the pan is small and deep; a larger, flatter pan will need careful watching to make sure the liquid doesn't boil away entirely! When the sauce is thickened, store in a tightly covered jar to cool thoroughly. Store in the refrigerator.

To serve, remove the chicken from the stock and dry it thoroughly. (Paper towels are handy.) Slice into thin long pieces and arrange on a serving dish. Save the most beautiful slices for the top of the mound. This is not dishonesty, just tact. Put slices of cucumbers around the chicken and pour the cold sauce over the chicken. Sprinkle the sauce with thin slices of scallion or snips of chives.

Both the chicken and the sauce should be cool but not icy. Let them moderate a bit if they have been stored in the refrigerator.

N.B. This dish makes fine hors d'ouevres, too. Cut the chicken in cubes instead of thin slices and impale each cube on a toothpick. The sauce is better poured over all at the beginning than used for a dip; it is a little intense as a dip.

*Start with a piece of ginger about 1″ long and ½″ in diameter and then taste. You will probably want to add 3 pieces this size or its equivalent in all; the sauce is *supposed* to be hot.

PEPPER CHICKEN

1 **white cut chicken or quick poached chicken (The larger bird will feed more people—or give you more leftovers.)**
30 **grains Szechuan pepper (or 1 2″ stick cinnamon or ½ teaspoon ground cinnamon)**
¼ **cup chicken fat (rendered or from the soup)**
¼ **cup soy sauce**
1 **teaspoon cayenne pepper or 3 chilis pequines, crushed**

Cut up the chicken, bones and all, into bite-sized pieces. Toast the Szechuan peppers in a skillet for a minute—do not let them scorch. Add oil and soy sauce and remove from the heat. Add cayenne or chilis pequines and pour sauce over chicken pieces.

If stick cinnamon is used, take it out before serving, of course. If the sauce tastes lively enough to you before adding the cayenne or chilis pequines, leave them out. Consider the group you're feeding: you want to intrigue them, not burn them!

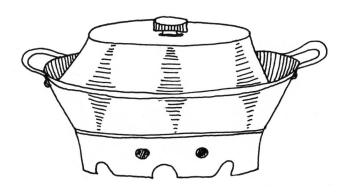

CHICKEN WITH PEANUTS

2 **whole raw chicken breasts**
1 **cup roasted, unsalted peanuts**
2 **teaspoons Szechuan peppercorns**
1 **teaspoon salt**
2 **tablespoons peanut oil**

Skin and bone the breasts and cut into thin slices. Cut the slices into 1″ squares and set aside.

Put the peanuts in a saucepan and add enough water barely to cover them, the peppercorns, roughly crushed, and the salt. Bring to a boil, then turn off the heat. Let the peanuts stand in the broth for 10 or 15 minutes. Drain them and dry well with paper towels. (If you can find only salted peanuts, and this does happen, rinse them under warm water before beginning the cooking process. Reduce or eliminate the 1 teaspoon salt.)

Just a few minutes before you plan to serve the dish, heat the oil in a heavy skillet. Add the chicken pieces to the pan and cook stirring constantly until they are just white. Stir in the peanuts for just long enough to heat through and become coated with the oil. Serve at once. Do not add salt or soy sauce; the dish is somewhat bland on purpose, though those peanuts have a mysterious punch.

HOT AND COLD MARINATED CHICKEN

  1 quick-poached chicken
  2 tablespoons oil
  2 teaspoons fresh ginger, minced
  2 tablespoons soy sauce
  1 tablespoon grated onion
½ teaspoon sugar
  6 Szechuan peppercorns, roughly crushed
  2 cloves garlic, minced
  1 or more hot green chilis or dried red chilis, to taste

Cool the chicken in its cooking broth. Cut into bite-sized pieces, bones and all, with a cleaver or a heavy knife and a mallet. Mix the rest of the ingredients. (Process them until smooth in a blender if you have one.) Put the cut-up chicken in a bowl and pour the marinade over it. Stir to coat all sides of the meat. Cover tightly and let stand an hour or two in the refrigerator. (Overnight won't hurt, but in that case, go easy on the chilis.)

The sauce should be quite hot, but let your taste be your guide; 1 or 2 chilis serranos or 8 chilis pequines will make a spirited sauce. Add them a little at a time and taste gingerly. Remember that more hotness will be absorbed by the chicken while it marinates than you will taste at once.

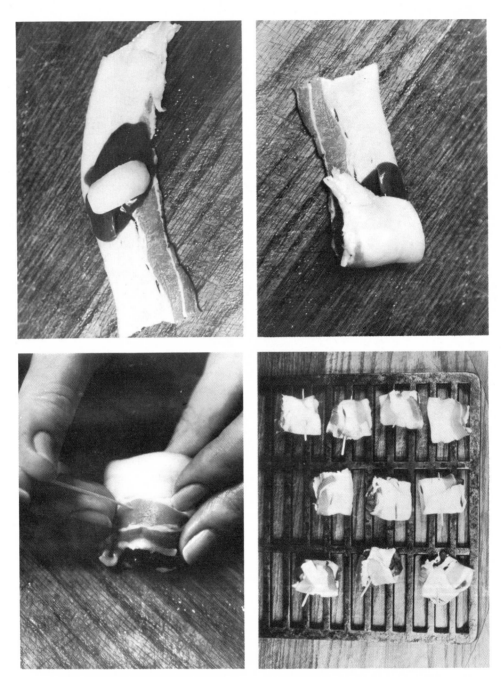

Rumaki

Bacon is much easier to roll if it is laid out on work surface. Fold ends of bacon over filling. Toothpick should go through water chestnut and liver.

CHICKEN LIVERS WITH BACON AND WATER CHESTNUTS (Rumaki)

½ pound chicken livers
½ pound bacon
 1 can water chestnuts

Drain the livers and dry them. Cut the bacon slices in half. Slice the water chestnuts in half, also. Count the bacon half slices; cut enough livers into thirds so that there will be one piece for each piece of bacon.

Place the bacon on a work surface. Lay the chicken liver in the middle of the bacon and half a water chestnut on top of the liver. Now fold first one end of the bacon, then the other over the liver and chestnut. Secure with a toothpick. This sounds harder than it is; if you work with fairly small pices of liver and chestnuts, you should have no trouble. The finished bundles will look rather sloppy, chances are, but do not worry. They are going to be broiled, about 3 inches from the flame, until both sides are browned. The bacon will contract while cooking to make the kabobs look quite neat. (Put them on a rack over a roasting pan to broil; a lot of fat cooks out of the bacon.)

The rumaki (actually an Indonesian dish*) may be made some time before it is to be broiled. In that case arrange the pieces on the rack and pan you plan to use, cover the whole arrangement tightly with foil, and refrigerate. Otherwise the livers will dry out and generally deteriorate.

These are splendid hot hors d'oeuvres, of course. No extra sauce or condiments are needed.

*Maybe—lots of cross-pollination from Chinese food in Indonesia.

Cold Chicken in Red Hot Oil

COLD CHICKEN IN RED HOT OIL

**breast and thighs from one frying chicken (You can use wing mauls and
drumsticks, too, if you need more meat.)**
1 cup peanut or sesame oil
**3 dried hot red peppers, whole, or 1 chili pasilla about 6 inches long, or
6 chilis pequines**

Poach the chicken pieces in unsalted water and let them cool in
the stock. Store in the refrigerator until ready to serve.

To make the oil, bring oil and chilis you are using (each variety
will give a slightly different taste, but each is good) to smoking
hot in a small saucepan. Remove from the heat and let cool. Pour
into a jar with a tight-fitting lid and store at room temperature until
ready to use, but at least 12 hours. The flavor and color of the
oil will develop and improve for several days, say 4 days; then
the oil should be stored in the refrigerator. It will continue to get
hotter as long as the chilis are left in it. You may want to taste
it after the first 12 hours and decide if you want to take the chilis
out then.

To serve, cut the chicken meat into long thin bite-sized slices
and toss with just enough oil to coat, as you would add salad dressing
to coat greens. You will probably have oil left over, but the 1 cup
is the best quantity to make easily—smaller amounts of oil burn
while heating too easily. You might also want to let guests add
their own oil if they are new to hot foods. Pass the soy sauce or
coarse salt at the table.

CHICKEN LIVERS WITH TREE EARS AND SCALLIONS

½ pound chicken livers
10 dried black Chinese mushrooms (or Italian mushrooms, dried)
6 to 10 scallions, depending on the size
1 tablespoon oil
¼ cup sherry
2 tablespoons soy sauce
1 teaspoon lemon juice or rice wine vinegar
  black pepper to taste

Drain and dry chicken livers. Soak mushrooms for 5 minutes in very hot water. Clean scallions and slice in ½" pieces (cut diagonally), green and all.

Heat oil in a skillet. Drain and dry mushrooms and slice them in ¼" slices. Cook just until tender, then push to one side of pan. Sauté the chicken livers and scallions together; turn the livers once so that both sides cook evenly.

When livers are just done, remove to serving dish. Mix sherry and soy sauce and pour into skillet with mushrooms and scallions. Stir to get up all the good bits that will stick to the skillet. Add lemon juice and pour sauce over livers. Serve at once. Pass the pepper grinder at the table.

N.B. Sweet vermouth is also very good in this recipe. And another variation is dry vermouth—also good with beef liver.

CHICKEN LIVERS WITH BAMBOO SHOOTS

½ pound chicken livers
1 cup bamboo shoots (Canned are fine.)
1 tablespoon oil or lard (Lard is better.)
  tiny pinch cinnamon
1 tablespoon orange marmalade or sweet liqueur

Drain and dry chicken livers. Drain bamboo shoots. Heat oil or lard in a skillet and sauté livers on both sides. Keep heat gentle and watch carefully so that they don't overcook. Add bamboo shoots and stir just to heat through. Sprinkle with cinnamon and add marmalade or liqueur. Cook just enough to coat livers and bamboo shoots with the sauce. Serve soy sauce to add to taste.

CHICKEN HEARTS AND GIZZARDS WITH VEGETABLES

½ **pound chicken hearts or gizzards or a mixture of both**
1 **cup thinly sliced white vegetable**
½ **cup thinly sliced dark green vegetable**
2 **tablespoons oil**
2 **tablespoons soy sauce**
2 **teaspoons dry mustard**
1 **teaspoon sugar**

Wash and dry chicken hearts. Wash gizzards and place in a saucepan. Barely cover with cold water and bring to a boil. Reduce heat so that broth simmers and cover pan. Poach until gizzards are almost tender. (A sharp knife should pierce them easily.) Remove gizzards and drain. When they are cool enough to handle, remove the tough whitish membrane—you will have two small pieces of meat from each gizzard. Cut each piece in half and slice each raw chicken heart in half lengthwise.

Prepare vegetables by peeling off tough outer skin (such as that on broccoli stems), then slicing thin. Cabbage, the hard center of bok choy (Chinese celery), celery, or bamboo shoots might be the light-colored vegetable; broccoli, spinach (in which case shred instead of slice), watercress, or string beans would make a pretty contrast.

Heat the oil in a large skillet. Add the dry chicken giblets and stir and cook quickly. Add the vegetables and just sprinkle with water. Cover tightly. When vegetables are crisp-tender, remove from heat. Mix soy sauce, mustard, and sugar and pour over meat and vegetables.

CHICKEN GIZZARDS WITH PEPPERS AND SPINACH

½ pound chicken gizzards
1 6″ chili pasilla
½ pound raw spinach
2 tablespoons oil
2 tablespoons soy sauce
½ teaspoon dry mustard

Wash and dry gizzards; remove tough membrane from each one so that two small pieces of meat are left. Slice each one into two pieces. Soak the chili pasilla in very hot water for 10 minutes. Drain and dry and slice in ¼″ slices. Remove and discard all the seeds. Wash and drain the spinach and remove any tough stems. Shred the leaves into ½″ pieces.

Heat the oil in a skillet. Add the gizzards and sauté until they are tender. Add the chili pasilla and stir so that it cooks on all sides. Meanwhile, mix the soy sauce and dry mustard. Add the spinach to the skillet, pour the soy sauce mixture over it, and tightly cover the pan. Reduce the heat at once and cook for 5 minutes. When the dish is ready to serve, the spinach should be wilted but still bright green. Stir the skillet well before placing the dish on a serving platter.

CRISP ROAST DUCK

 1 **duck, about 6 pounds**
 ¼ **cup soy sauce**
 ½ **cup lemon juice or rice wine vinegar**
 2 **tablespoons honey**
 2 **tablespoons brown sugar**
 1 **teaspoon salt**

Clean and wash the duck and dry it. Truss if it is to be served whole. Cut it into serving pieces otherwise. (The smaller pieces are easier to handle.) Place the duck on the rack of a steamer and steam until the meat is fork-tender; check in 35 minutes and often thereafter. When it is done, remove from steamer and dry well. Place in the refrigerator until it is very cold. (Using the freezer will speed this step up somewhat, but allow enough time for the duck to get *cold*.)

About an hour before cooking, remove duck from the refrigerator. Mix the rest of the ingredients together and brush well over the duck. Let dry 10 minutes or so, then brush again. Repeat as long as there is time and liquid left. To cook, heat the oven to 550° F. Place the glazed duck on a rack over a roasting pan and place in the oven. Do not add oil—the duck will still have plenty of its skin to baste itself. Watch the duck carefully; it will be done when the skin is very crisp and quite dark. Don't let it burn, though; it will go from very dark brown (just right) to black (burned) fast indeed.

HOT MARINATED FRIED DUCK

   breast and legs from a 6-pound duck
 1 **tablespoon soy sauce**
 1 **teaspoon salt**
¼ **cup sweet sherry**
 1 **medium onion, thinly sliced**
 2 **cloves garlic, minced**
 2 **chilis serranos or Italian hot green peppers**
 1 **piece fresh ginger about 1″ × ½″, sliced or minced**
 2 **egg yolks or 1 whole egg, slightly beaten**
½ **cup cornstarch**
¼ **cup lard or oil (Lard is better.)**

Wash duck; leave skin on. Split the breast and divide legs into thighs and drumsticks.

Mix soy sauce, salt, sherry, onion, peppers, and ginger together and marinate the duck overnight in the refrigerator.

To cook, drain and dry the duck pieces. Mix together the eggs, ¼ cup water, and enough cornstarch to give a thick paste. Spread over one side of the duck pieces and let dry 10 minutes; turn and repeat. (Put the battered side of the duck on a plate or piece of waxed paper sprinkled with the rest of the cornstarch so it won't stick or be disturbed.) Heat the lard in a skillet. When it is smoking hot, add the duck. Do not crowd; do it in several batches if necessary. Turn after 2 minutes and immediately reduce the heat. Turn again after 4 minutes and cook until duck is very tender, turning once again; allow about 10 minutes on each side. Cut into bite-sized serving pieces and make sure that each person gets some breast and some leg meat. Pass the pepper grinder at the table.

Basic Duck

BASIC DUCK (Red Cooked Duck)

 1 **duck, about 6 pounds**
 ½ **cup soy sauce**
 ¼ **cup sweet sherry**
 2 **scallions or 1 medium onion, sliced**

Leave the duck whole or cut it into serving pieces. Place in a pan with a tight-fitting lid and half cover it with cold water. Bring the liquid to a boil, then add the rest of the ingredients. Cook briskly for 10 minutes, then reduce heat to simmering and cover pan. Check for tenderness in 45 minutes. Duck should be quite tender and slightly drawing away from its bones. A whole duck will take longer than a cut-up one, of course.

   Duck is usually served hot. The basic dish would be the cooked duck cut into bite-sized pieces and served with the cooking liquid, skimmed of all fat, thickened with a little cornstarch or not, as you please. Unthickened broth is more authentic and probably better for you!

DUCK MARINATED WITH FRUIT AND RED WINE

- 1 duck, about 6 pounds
- 2 cups *good* dry red wine, Burgundy or claret, perhaps
- 1 tart red apple, cored but not peeled, diced
- ½ cup dried apricots cut in thin slices
- 2 tablespoons orange rind cut in slivers
- 6 seeded raw prunes
- 1 teaspoon salt
- ¼ cup brown sugar
- 1 medium onion, sliced roughly
- 2 whole cloves
- 6 Szechuan peppercorns or white peppercorns roughly crushed

Cut the duck into serving pieces. Wipe with a damp cloth.

In some dishes it doesn't matter much whether wine used in cooking is of excellent quality or not; in this one it does. Mix the wine and the rest of the ingredients and pour the marinade over the duck in a glass or porcelain bowl. Allow to marinate in the refrigerator 1 or 2 days. Stir once in a while to make sure all the duck is in contact with the wine mixture, but keep it tightly covered the rest of the time.

When ready to cook, drain and dry the duck pieces. Save the marinade. Dredge the duck in flour and fry (see Hot Marinated Fried Duck for times) until tender. While the duck cooks, remove the prunes from the marinade and cut them about the size of the apple pieces. Taste the marinade; add soy sauce, water, more sugar, slivers of lemon peel, whatever pleases your taste. Heat and reduce to about half. Pass at the table with the duck.

FISH
&
SEAFOOD

FISH
&
SEAFOOD

Hunan is an inland province and until modern times simply did not have seafoods in its cuisine. Freshwater fish are plentiful, however, and many of the varieties used in China are available here. The kind of flesh the fish has and its size are more important than its variety—and the names change from place to place so much that it is often difficult to know if your carp is another man's carp. Any nonfatty white-fleshed fish will do nicely for the fish recipes following: bass, carp, perch, or trout.

Dried shrimp are not perishable and so were available inland before the days of refrigeration and fast transportation. They are available here in Chinese groceries. Perhaps you could persuade your market to stock them, too. They can be used in all the shrimp recipes after they have been soaked in hot water to restore their freshness. Plan to soak at least 30 minutes; an hour would be better. Then rinse in cold water, dry, and proceed with the recipe.

Though seafood is not traditional in Hunan cooking, there is no reason why you shouldn't use the sauces and combinations given in this book for Hunan-*style* dishes. Lobster meat is very good in all the fresh-fish recipes, and it works fine in the chicken recipes, too. Bay scallops, saltwater fish fillets, and crabmeat also taste good Hunan style.

SHRIMP WITH VEGETABLES

½ **pound fresh raw shrimp**
 1 **cup broccoli flowerets**
12 **tiny white carrots or ½ cup bamboo shoots or water chestnuts or thinly sliced hearts of bok choy**
 1 **teaspoon oil**
½ **cup unsalted chicken broth or water**
 2 **teaspoons cornstarch**
 1 **teaspoon salt**
½ **teaspoon white pepper**

Wash and shell the shrimp. Wash and thoroughly dry the broccoli. Drain the carrots (they come canned) and dry with paper towels.

Heat oil in a skillet. Add broccoli and toss to coat thoroughly. Cook 1 minute over medium heat. Add chicken broth just to cover the bottom of the skillet. Cover tightly and cook 2 minutes. Check broccoli; it should be barely tender and still bright green. (If bok choy or other raw vegetable is used, add it at the same time the broccoli is put in the skillet and increase the oil to 2 teaspoons.) Add the shrimp to the skillet and again add just enough broth to keep pan moist. Cover and cook 1 minute. The shrimp should be barely opaque. While the shrimp cooks, mix cornstarch with salt, pepper, and the remaining broth. When shrimp is barely done, pour sauce mixture into pan and stir briskly until it is thickened and coats shrimp and vegetables. Add carrots just to heat through and take on a coating of sauce. Serve at once.

SHRIMP WITH SWEET AND HOT GREEN PEPPERS

½ pound fresh raw shrimp
1 large or 2 small green bell peppers
1 small hot pepper (chili serrano or Italian hot green pepper)
1 tablespoon oil
1 tablespoon soy sauce
½ teaspoon sugar
½ teaspoon cornstarch (optional)

Clean and shell the shrimp and dry it thoroughly. Seed the green bell pepper and cut it into thin slivers. Split the hot green pepper and remove all seeds and discard them. Mince the hot pepper.

Heat oil in a skillet. Put the bell pepper in the pan and stir to coat with oil. Cover the pan and cook 2 minutes. The pepper should be barely tender but still bright green. Add the shrimp and the hot pepper to the skillet. Stir to coat with oil and cover. Cook 1 minute. The shrimp should be only barely opaque.

While the shrimp cooks, mix the soy sauce, sugar, and cornstarch. Pour over shrimp and peppers and stir to cook only until sauce thickens and coats them.

If you decide not to use cornstarch, cook both the bell pepper and the shrimp a bit less (about 15 seconds) and let the unthickened sauce cook a little more. It will not be as thick, but it will taste fine.

N.B. Lobster, scallops, or other shellfish would be good in this dish, too. Just make sure they aren't cooked to death.

Red Hot Shrimp

RED HOT SHRIMP

½ pound shrimp
10 chilis pequines
2 tablespoons oil
1 clove garlic, minced
    salt to taste

Clean the shrimp and set aside. If you are using dried shrimp, soak in hot water until tender; drain and set aside. In a very heavy pan with a tight lid, place the chilis and the oil. Heat gently so that the chilis toast but do not burn. When they are brown, add the garlic and stir for 1 minute.*

Add the shrimp to the pan. If they are raw, stir well to coat them with oil, then cover the pan tightly and reduce heat as much as possible. Cook 1 minute, then check on shrimp. They should be barely opaque. If dried reconstituted shrimp are used, stir and heat just enough to be sure they are warm through. Put the shrimp on a serving dish and pour any oil left in the pan over them. Serve at once and eat hot; this dish is not susceptible to being a leftover.

*There is something to be said for removing the chilis at this point. Let your taste and your diners be your guide.

CHICKEN-FAT FISH

1 4-pound white-fleshed fish
1 piece of fresh ginger about 1½″ × ½″
2 cloves garlic, peeled
6 scallions or 1 medium onion, diced
4 tablespoons rendered chicken fat
2 hot green chilis, such as chili serrano or Italian green chili
3 tablespoons soy sauce
1 teaspoon sugar
  about 2 cups unsalted chicken broth, heated to boiling

Rinse the whole fish and dry it well inside and out. Sprinkle with a little salt and rub it well into the skin. Mince the ginger and garlic fine or run them through the blender until they are well chopped. Cut the scallions or onion roughly.

Heat the chicken fat in a large skillet. Add the chilis and let them cook over medium heat until they are wilted; remove from pan and set aside. Add ginger, garlic, scallions, soy sauce, and sugar to the skillet. When the scallions are wilted, turn up the heat and place the fish in the skillet. Brown on both sides, then add the hot chicken broth just to cover the fish. Reduce the heat at once and simmer the fish, covered tightly, until it is barely tender, about 8 minutes. Remove the fish to a serving platter and keep warm.

Taste the sauce; if it is hot enough, discard the hot peppers. Otherwise, return them, or part of them, to the pan and increase the heat so that the sauce reduces and slightly thickens. A teaspoon of cornstarch mixed with a little cold water may be used to thicken the sauce, but it will be better plain.

Bean curd is a traditional accompaniment for Chicken-Fat Fish. If you can get it, cut about 1½ cups into small sqares and add to the sauce when the fish is removed from the pan. If it is not available, as is the case very often in the United States, reduce the sauce and pour it over the fish and serve. Broad noodles make an unorthodox but tasty fill-in for the bean curd but serve them around the fish, not in the sauce.

COLD POACHED FISH WITH GINGER AND GARLIC SAUCE

2 fillets, about ½ pound, of firm white-fleshed fish
  unsalted chicken broth or water just to cover fish
  ginger and garlic sauce (See recipe for Cold Chicken with Fresh Ginger
  and Garlic Sauce.)
1 whole scallion, chopped
  watercress for garnish

Poach the fish gently until just done. Cool in the broth and chill thoroughly. Make the ginger and garlic sauce and let it get cold.

To serve, break the fish into bite-sized pieces, not too small, and arrange on a serving dish. Pour the sauce over the fish, then sprinkle the sauce with the chopped scallion. Decorate the platter with watercress.

The fish is too fragile to be served as finger food, but a very good appetizer or cocktail snack would be as follows:

COLD SHRIMP WITH FRESH GINGER AND GARLIC SAUCE

½ pound raw shrimp
  ginger and garlic sauce (See recipe for Cold Chicken with Fresh Ginger and
  Garlic Sauce.)
  minced parsley

Clean and cook the shrimp just until it is opaque. Drain and cool, tightly covered. Or use dried shrimp; soak them in very hot water until they are plump and tender, then drain and chill.

Make and cool the ginger and garlic sauce. Serve the shrimp on a platter covered with the sauce for a main dish; impale them on toothpicks and sprinkle with minced parsley for hors d'oeuvres. Use the sauce as a dip.

SHRIMP WITH CASHEWS

½ pound fairly small raw shrimp*
½ pound unsalted cashews†
 1 teaspoon peanut oil
 1 teaspoon cornstarch or rice starch
   pinch freshly ground dried ginger root

Shell and clean the shrimp; set aside.

Place the cashews in a saucepan and barely cover them with water. Bring to a boil. Immediately remove the nuts with a slotted spoon and place in a colander to drain. Cover with a towel to keep warm. Put the shrimp into the boiling water and turn the heat off *at once*. Cover the pan and wait *1 minute*. The shrimp should then be just opaque and tender. Do not overcook. Lift the shrimp from the water with a slotted spoon and drain them. Combine shrimp and cashews in the top of a double boiler and keep them warm over warm, not boiling, water while the sauce is made.

Measure ¼ cup of the cooking liquid and combine it with the cornstarch and ginger. Bring to a boil and simmer, stirring, until it is thickened. This will take only a minute or so. Very gently stir just enough sauce into the shrimp and cashews to moisten them and give them a glossy coating. Serve at once. Do not add salt; this dish is bland on purpose. You will very much appreciate it as a break from spicy dishes.

*If frozen shrimp only are available, use them. Do not cover; watch very carefully. Remove from heat and rinse with cold water as soon as they are opaque.

†If only salted nuts are available, wash them.

SAUTÉED WHOLE FISH

This is a basic recipe—it may be thought of as a first step in preparing many Chinese dishes.

1 **white-fleshed fish, about 4 pounds**
½ **cup flour, cornstarch, or rice starch**
    lard or oil for frying

Wash and dry the fish; leave the head, tail, and fins on. Sift enough flour over the fish to coat it well, then shake to remove the excess flour.

Meanwhile, heat enough lard or oil in a skillet large enough to hold the fish to make the fat 1″ deep. If you have a frying thermometer, now is the time to use it: heat the fat to 360° F. If you do not have a thermometer, heat the fat over a brisk fire until it is hot but not smoking. Put the fish in the skillet and cook about a minute on each side. Turn the heat down and cook another 5 or 6 minutes, turning once. The fish is ready to remove when a meat thermometer inserted in the thickest part of the flesh registers 145° F. If you do not have a thermometer, time the fish carefully and remove it when it is just browned nicely and before the fish "flakes," a sign that it is already overdone. It will continue to cook even after it is removed from the hot oil. A fish that is to be eaten plain, with soy sauce as seasoning and some sautéed vegetables on the side, needs a little more cooking than one to be reheated with sauce. Rescue the one to be reused as soon as it is a nice color.

FISH WITH BROWN SAUCE

1 whole sautéed 4-pound fish (see Sautéed Whole Fish)
1 cup unsalted chicken stock or water
3 tablespoons soy sauce
¼ teaspoon dry mustard
¾ teaspoon sugar
1 piece of fresh ginger about 3″ × ½″
4 cloves of garlic, peeled
watercress or other greens for garnish

Prepare the fish and set aside.

Combine the rest of the ingredients except the garnish in a blender and process until smooth.* Pour into a saucepan and bring to a boil, then reduce the heat so the sauce simmers. Cook until it is quite thick. This takes some time and patience; the heat has to be low so that the mixture doesn't burn. Stir often and remove from heat when it is the consistency of thin hollandaise sauce.

When the sauce just begins to thicken, reheat the fish in hot fat just until it is warm through. Drain well, place on a serving platter, and dress with the sauce when it is thick. Garnish with watercress and serve at once. This dish really does have to be served hot, though any leftovers are good.

*If you do not have a blender, cut the ginger and garlic into small pieces and crush them to paste with a mortar and pestle. The blender is easier.

Fish with Brown Sauce (page 67)

PLAIN STEAMED FISH

1 4-pound white-fleshed fish
1 tablespoon soy sauce
1 tablespoon sherry
1 piece of fresh ginger about 1″ × ½″ (optional)
1 slice onion
   water barely to cover fish

To steam a fish, it is necessary to have a steamer that will hold both the fish and its interior pan. A large double boiler will do, or better yet a clam steamer or some other pot of that size with a rack to hold the interior pan and the fish. If the fish is a close fit, skewer it and bend it a bit. (This will give a faint appearance of swimming if your imagination is very good.) The bending may make it fit.

Clean and dry the whole fish. Mix the soy sauce, sherry, ginger, and onion in the interior bowl or pan or the top of the double boiler. Place the fish in the interior bowl and add just enough hot water to cover it. Place the bowl in the steamer (or over the bottom of the double boiler), which has 2″ of water boiling in it. Cover tightly and steam until the fish is barely cooked, 145° F. on a meat thermometer inserted in the thickest part of the flesh, about 25 minutes. Check often as steaming time comes to an end. Do not overcook the fish. Serve at once; pass the soy sauce. (New soy sauce, that is—the cooking liquid has served its purpose.)

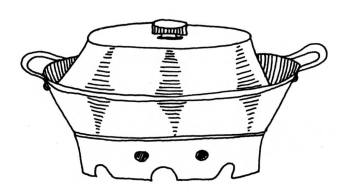

BEEF
&
PORK

BEEF
&
PORK

Pork and beef are both used in Hunan much more than in Canton, the city with whose cuisine most people in the West are most familiar. When *meat* is referred to in China, though, it means *pork*. Not only is pork more available, its texture is more highly thought of. It cooks tenderer with less fuss than beef, too.

Most of the recipes listed for pork can be made with beef and vice versa. One exception is meatballs; beef meatballs will not taste at all like the pork ones and will be tougher besides. Stick to pork for meatballs.

It is important that all pork be thoroughly cooked to avoid the danger of trichinosis. Do not taste raw pork while you are cooking—taste sausage mixtures by frying a tiny dab, then tasting that. It is not difficult to cook pork well without overcooking it: A meat thermometer (an excellent investment) will register 145° F. when it is done and perfectly safe. If you do not have a thermometer, cook pork until it loses its pink color, which happens at 150° F. Pork slices, shreds, and minced pork cook very, very fast, of course, because the pieces are so small. Do not overcook them; they won't be as delicious or as tender if you do.

BASIC BOILED PORK, WHOLE

1 whole fresh shoulder or ham, about 6 pounds, skin on and bone in
2 cups water
3 tablespoons sweet sherry
1 tablespoon sugar
1 tablespoon honey
1 cup soy sauce
1 piece fresh ginger about 1″ × ½″, sliced

Wash and dry the shoulder or ham. Place it, fat side down, in a heavy pot with a tight-fitting lid. Place over medium heat and cook until a little of the fat has rendered out. While the lean side is up, puncture it in several places with a skewer or a thin sharp knife. Turn the meat fat side up and add the water. Bring to a boil, add the other ingredients, cover and reduce the heat so that the liquid simmers. Cook very slowly until the meat is tender, about 2 hours. Test for doneness often if the meat is not tender at the end of 2 hours; you don't want to overcook it. Serve hot or cold.

BASIC BOILED PORK, CUT UP

To cook pieces of pork, cut them into 1½″ cubes; for 3 or 4 pounds of pork, reduce the water to 1 cup, the soy sauce to ½ cup, and eliminate the honey. Cook the same way as for whole shoulder or ham until the meat is tender, about 1 hour.

BASIC SHREDDED PORK

½ **pound lean boneless pork**
2 **teaspoons soy sauce**
2 **teaspoons sweet sherry**

Wipe the pork with a damp cloth or paper towels; dry thoroughly. Slice very thin, as for pork slices, then cut each slice again to make very thin shreds. The pieces of meat should be about $^1/_{16}''$ × $^1/_{16}''$ × 1". Mix the pork with soy sauce, sherry, and a little salt, if desired.

This is the basic recipe for shredded pork dishes. The meat is not served alone usually, but vegetables and flavorings are added during the cooking process. The pork takes only 2 minutes of stir frying to cook done; be sure to have other ingredients on hand and prepared. Add them before, during, or after the meat according to the time they require.

PORK SHREDS WITH BOK CHOY

A popular shredded pork dish combines the meat with this crisp light-and-dark vegetable.

Wash and thoroughly dry ½ a head of bok choy. Slice the dark green tops in shreds ¼"; peel the white base if necessary and cut into shreds about the same size as the pork shreds. (If you have it, the heart of the bok choy head is very good; cut it even finer than the white part of the stems.)

Heat 1 tablespoon lard in a heavy skillet. Put the stems and heart of the bok choy into the fat and stir fry for 30 seconds. Add the pork and cook for another 30 seconds. Add the dark green bok choy tops, 1 teaspoon soy sauce, ½ teaspoon salt, and ¼ teaspoon dry mustard to the skillet and cook 1 minute more, stirring constantly. Serve at once.

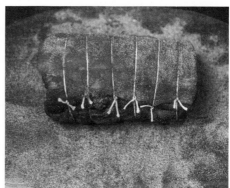

Bone the meat and rub spices thoroughly on outside and inside the bone cavity. Tie the meat so it will keep its shape during curing. Pack in crockery container and cover with salt.

HOT DRY-MARINATED PORK

To cure pork in this way, two things are needed that you must be sure to have on hand: time—about a week or 10 days at least—and an earthenware container large enough to hold the cut of pork being cured.

1 loin of pork, at least 4 pounds, or 1 fresh pork shoulder or part of one
weighing at least 4 pounds
2 tablespoons (or more) Szechuan peppercorns, coarsely ground
1 small can cayenne pepper, about 1½ to 2 ounces
1 26-ounce box plain table salt (This is the usual size.)

Bone the pork you plan to cure or ask the butcher to do it for you. (Make sure he gives you the bones for soup.) Wipe the meat inside and out with a damp cloth or paper towels and dry thoroughly. Rub the bone cavity *very* well with the Szechuan pepper. Use more if it is needed; the cavity should be well covered. Rub it in. Rub the cavity thoroughly with salt now as well.

Re-form the meat and tie up tightly with butcher's twine. Mix the cayenne pepper with about a third of the salt left in the box. Rub the mixture very well into all the outside surfaces of the meat, being especially careful that the fat as well as the lean spots are well covered. Place a layer of salt-pepper mixture in the bottom of the container in which the meat is to cure. Put the meat in (it should be a tight fit) and fill up any air spaces with salt; plan to use the whole box. Tightly cover the container with a double layer of heavy-duty aluminum foil and tie it securely. If the container has a lid, place it on top of the foil; it will protect it while the meat cures.

If you have a very cool pantry (and the weather is good and cold) or a smokehouse or an outside porch, the pork can marinate outside the refrigerator. If there is any doubt, put the jar in the refrigerator. Let it stay, undistrubed, for at least a week.

When ready to cook the pork, remove it from the container and let it begin coming to room temperature. Wash it well in cold water to remove the excess salt and red cayenne pepper (scrub around the securing strings especially), then dry it well. Heat the oven to 300° F. Place the pork on a rack over a roasting pan and lay some slices of uncured fat pork over the meat if its own fat is thin. Roast until a meat thermometer registers 145° F., about 25 minutes per pound. (This time will vary with the shape of the meat—the flatish loin will cook faster than the shoulder.) When the roast is done, let it stand 15 minutes before carving. Thicken the pan drippings with a little cornstarch, season with soy sauce, and add water to make gravy, if desired. Slice and serve hot or cold or use in twice-cooked pork recipes.

N.B. Working with the hot peppers can make your hands burn. If your skin is sensitive or if the skin is broken, wear rubber gloves. Holding smarting fingers in a bowl of salt or in strong cold brine (2 tablespoons salt in 1 cup water) helps if you do get hot fingers.

HOT PEPPER MINCED PORK

½ **pound minced raw pork (See Basic Minced Pork, page 82)**
1 **green bell pepper**
1 **red bell pepper**
3 **cloves garlic**
6 **chilis pequines**
2 **tablespoons minced unsalted, unsmoked bacon, or lard**
4 **tablespoons soy sauce**
1 **teaspoon wine vinegar**
2 **teaspoons sugar or sweet sherry**

Mince the pork and set aside. Seed the bell peppers and dice them into ½" pieces. Peel and mince the garlic and add it along with the chilis to a heavy skillet with the bacon or lard. Cook over medium heat for 2 minutes; do not let the garlic or the chilis burn.* Add the bell peppers and cook 1 minute. Add the minced pork then and cook, stirring and breaking up lumps, for 2 minutes. Add soy sauce, vinegar, and sherry and cook one more minute, stirring constantly. Serve with flour pancakes.

*If you prefer a not-so-hot dish, remove the chilis at this point and discard them.

MEATBALLS AND CABBAGE

2 cups shredded (¼″ strips) white cabbage (Slice the heart thin if it is used.)
¼ cup water
1 teaspoon lard
1 tablespoon soy sauce
¼ teaspoon sugar
1 recipe Basic Minced Pork meatballs

Place the cabbage in a heavy pan with a tight lid. Add the rest of the ingredients except the meatballs and bring to a boil. Place the meatballs on top of the cabbage and cover the pot tightly. Reduce the heat so that the cabbage just simmers. Check the cabbage in 10 minutes; it should be just crisp-tender.

STUFFED HOT PEPPERS

½ a recipe for Basic Minced Pork, raw
1 tablespoon grated onion
1 tablespoon raisins or currants
¼ teaspoon cinnamon
4 bell peppers or mildly hot green peppers (chilis poblanos)

Mix onion and raisins with the minced pork and seasonings. Cook 2 minutes over medium heat in a heavy skillet, stirring constantly. Set aside.

Carefully cut into the peppers and remove all the seeds and membranes. Taste the chili poblano seeds; usually the peppers are mild, but sometimes a hot one appears. If one seems unbearably hot, use it for flavoring in cooking another dish and look for a milder one to stuff. On the other hand, if the peppers are relentlessly bland, or if you are using bell peppers, consider adding ½ teaspoon crushed or ground hot dried pepper to the filling.

Stuff the peppers and tie them or skewer them with toothpicks so they will keep their shape. Cook by steaming for 1 hour or poaching in broth deep enough to half cover for 30 minutes. Both preparation and cooking can be done ahead of time. Just reheat stuffed chilis by steaming or in a slow oven before serving.

Ingredients for Basic Stir-Fry Pork Slices

BASIC STIR-FRY PORK SLICES

½ **pound lean boneless pork**
1 **tablespoon soy sauce**
2 **teaspoons dry sherry**
1½ **teaspoons cornstarch (optional)**
1 **tablespoon water**
1 **tablespoon lard**

Cut the pork into very thin slices across the grain, then cut each slice into 2″ × 1″ pieces. Mix with the soy sauce, sherry, cornstarch, and water and toss to coat thoroughly.

Heat the lard in a heavy skillet.

This is the recipe for the meat portion of many dishes. The pork slices cooked by themselves make very nice cocktail tidbits. (Sprinkle them very discreetly with some cayenne pepper or a little Tabasco.) If the meat is to be combined with vegetables or whatever, the rest of the preparation depends on the other materials used. Add vegetables, cut in small, thin pieces, so that they will be just crisp-tender when the pork is done—3 minutes. Seasonings that need to heat go in at the beginning of the dish, the others just long enough to be mixed into the meat and vegetables. A popular hot sliced-pork dish features three kinds of peppers:

SLICED PORK WITH SWEET AND HOT PEPPERS

Soak 1 7″ chili pasilla in hot water for 10 minutes; seed and slice thinly crosswise. Slice ½ a red bell pepper and ½ a green bell pepper into ⅛″ slivers. Sauté the chili pasilla in 1 tablespoon of lard for 1 minute. Remove it from the pan and set aside. Add 1 teaspoon of lard to the skillet and put the pork slices in. Cook, stirring constantly, for 2 minutes. Add the bell peppers and the chili pasilla and stir fry for 1 more minute. Serve at once.

BASIC MINCED (GROUND) PORK

1 **pound boneless pork with some fat on it, such as fatty pork chops or shoulder**
1 **tablespoon soy sauce**
1 **teaspoon sweet sherry**
1 **teaspoon sugar**
2 **tablespoon cornstarch**
¼ **teaspoon salt**
½ **teaspoon white pepper**

Wipe the pork with a damp cloth; remove all tough fibers and ligaments. Mince finely. Traditionally 2 1-pound cleavers are used for mincing, but with patience you can mince pork with a sharp knife. Begin by slicing it very thin, then shredding the slices, then chopping the shreds. The pork should not be gooey but should retain the look of small pieces of meat. The mixture should be quite light pink; if it is not, add some more fat and chop it in.

It is also possible to grind the pork, though it won't have quite the same character as hand-minced meat and may tend to shrink more in cooking. Chill both the meat and the meat grinder thoroughly. (If the butcher grinds the pork for you, he should have his grinder in the cold room; if he doesn't, find another butcher.) Cut the pork into cubes that will fit the grinder intake easily. Grind quickly, using a coarse or medium blade. Put the ground meat back in the refrigerator at once; dismantle the grinder and *wash it thoroughly* in very hot water and soap to eliminate the danger of contaminating other foods ground in it with trichinosis.

Mix the minced pork with the rest of the ingredients and stir to combine thoroughly. Form the sausage into meatballs or small patties, depending on how they are to be used. Heat enough lard in a heavy skillet to give a ¼" hot fat. Fry over medium heat, turning to brown on all sides, about 5 minutes in all (less time for tiny meatballs).

Meatballs can be served either hot or cold as a meat accompaniment for vegetable dishes. In that case, serve a mixture of half salt, half freshly ground black pepper for each diner to dip into. Tiny meatballs are excellent hors d'oeuvres.

Meatballs and patties can also be used in an endless variety of combinations with vegetables. The method of preparing the dishes follows the pattern for sliced or shredded pork, except for minced pork the meat is mostly cooked and the vegetables are steamed. A few combinations are given as examples.

MEATBALLS AND BOK CHOY

2 cups shredded (1″ strips) bok choy
3 tablespoons water
2 teaspoons soy sauce
½ teaspoon salt
1 recipe Basic Minced Pork meatballs (about 6)

Place the bok choy, water, soy sauce, and salt in a heavy pan with a tight-fitting lid. Arrange the meatballs on top of the vegetable. Bring the pot to a boil, quickly cover, and reduce heat so that the pot simmers. Check the bok choy for tenderness in 8 minutes; steam another minute or two if it is not tender.

Meatballs that are to be used in these dishes can be cooked a shorter time than the ones to be eaten plain, but it is not all that important. If the pork used has enough fat, the meatballs will be tender and juicy.

Pork Shreds with Peppers

PORK SHREDS WITH PEPPERS

Cut 2 chilis serranos or hot green Italian chilis open and remove the seeds. Discard them and chop the hot chilis very fine. Shred ½ a red bell pepper and ½ a green bell pepper in ⅛″ pieces. Heat 1 tablespoon lard in a heavy skillet. Add the pork shreds and cook 1 minute, stirring constantly. Add the hot and sweet peppers and cook 1 minute more, still stirring. Add 1 teaspoon soy sauce and stir to mix thoroughly. Serve at once.

Dried hot chilis could be used in this recipe as well, but they seem to be even hotter and tend to swamp the delicate pork shreds.

Lions' Heads

LIONS' HEADS

The city of Yangchow (a man who had lived there said of the people, "They know how to *Live!*") contributes this dish, which is also popular in Hunan and Szechuan.

> 1 recipe Basic Minced Pork with the meat cut in slightly larger pieces or ground with a very coarse blade
> broth (chicken or pork or whatever you have) seasoned with a little soy sauce, depending on how salty the broth is, for poaching
> ½ head bok choy

Mix the minced pork and form into 4 large balls; they should be about the size of good-sized peaches. Meanwhile, heat the broth in a large pot (wide, not necessarily deep) until it is just boiling. Remove from the heat and very carefully put the lions' heads into the liquid. Cover the pot and let it stand 5 minutes. Return to heat, watching carefully, and let the liquid just simmer. Cook covered for 15 minutes without disturbing, then check. The meatballs—the Lions' Heads—should be almost done. When they are done (a meat thermometer removes the guesswork—145° F. is done), take them out of the broth and cook it hard to reduce it to ½ cup. Cut the bok choy into 1″ shreds and place in the broth. Very carefully arrange the lions' heads on the bok choy. Bring the liquid to a boil, then reduce heat so it just simmers. Cover the pot and cook for about 10 minutes, or until the bok choy is tender-crisp. Serve hot or cold with a little soy sauce and rice vinegar mixed.

Lions' heads may be sautéed, also. Use enough oil to make 1″ in the skillet and keep the heat moderate to low. Let the lions' heads cook until they are brown on all sides, turning only when one spot is brown. This will take 20 to 30 minutes. The crust is nice but the poaching is easier.

This is the extremely simplified version of the traditional recipe. For the real thing, see Yang Chow Lion's Head in *The Joy of Chinese Cooking* by Doreen Yen Hung Feng, Grosset & Dunlap, New York.

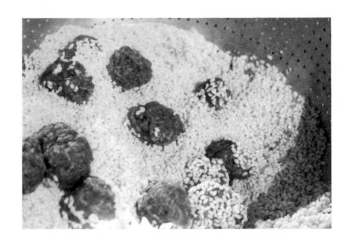

Pearl Balls

PEARL BALLS

1 recipe Basic Minced Pork, mixed but raw
2 tablespoons minced onion
2 cups raw rice

Mix the minced pork, seasonings, and onion together. Put the rice with water to cover generously in a heavy pan and bring to a boil. Reduce heat and cover; simmer until the outside of the rice grains is transparent, about 15 minutes. Drain the rice and rinse it with cold water; drain again.

Put the rice in a wide shallow bowl. Form 1″ balls from the pork mixture and roll them quickly in the rice, pressing gently so the grains stick to the meat. The meatballs may be made and coated with rice in advance. Just store them in the refrigerator until you are ready to cook them.

To cook, heat oil for deep frying to 360° F. and cook a few pearl balls at a time; do not crowd. Turn once or twice to make sure all sides cook evenly. Drain on paper towels and serve hot. Pass hot mustard and soy sauce.

RED HOT AND SWEET RIBS

- **2 pounds spareribs cut in 1″ slices (Separate the bones yourself so that you have bite-sized pieces.)**
- **6 chilis pequines or 1 chili ancho**
- **2 teaspoons sugar**
- **½ cup cornstarch or rice flour**
- **1 teaspoon cider vinegar**

Wipe the rib pieces with a damp cloth and place on a rack over an inch or two of water in a steamer. Bring water to a boil, reduce heat, and cover steamer. Cook for 30 minutes.

Let the riblets cool. When they are cool enough to handle, remove them from the steamer. If chilis pequines are used, toast them in a skillet until they are dark brown but do not let them burn. If dried chili ancho is used, soak it in hot water for 10 minutes, then carefully seed it and discard the seeds. Taste the chili ancho gingerly; it should be slightly hot but very flavorful, but sometimes it is hot, hot, hot. If it is *very* bland, add some hotter pepper, such as ground Szechuan peppercorns, Tabasco, or cayenne, to the dish.

Mix the pepper or chilis to be used with the sugar and grind them to powder in a mortar. Add the cornstarch and vinegar and just enough water to make a stiff paste (wear gloves if your hands are sensitive or have the skin broken—this mixture smarts!) and rub thoroughly into the riblets. Place on a rack above an inch of water in a steamer, bring the water to a boil, then reduce the heat. Cover and cook until the ribs are very tender, about 15 to 20 minutes more. Serve hot with soy sauce and ground salt.

BASIC PIG'S FEET

1 **whole pig's foot for each person to be served (Cook some extra—the soup is wonderful.)**
   water barely to cover feet
½ **cup soy sauce**
1 **teaspoon salt**
¼ **cup sweet sherry**
1 **piece fresh ginger 1″ × ½″, sliced**

Wash the feet thoroughly; split them in half lengthwise with a cleaver or a heavy knife and a mallet. Heat a large heavy pot with a tight lid; place the dried feet in it and cook over moderate heat until browned on all sides. (Enough fat will cook out of the feet to brown them.) Do not crowd; cook in several batches if necessary.

When all the pieces are browned, return them to the pot and add the rest of the ingredients. Cover and reduce heat so the liquid barely simmers. Test after 2 hours; the feet should be very tender. Simmer longer, tightly covered, if necessary.

To serve, place a whole foot (2 halves) on each diner's plate. Strain the cooking liquid and serve separately as sauce. Also provide grated horseradish, hot mustard, fresh ground black pepper, and soy sauce for dipping.

Bok choy or white or red cabbage, sauerkraut, or salted cabbage are particularly good with pig's feet. Shred the raw vegetable and toss in a little oil in a skillet. Add a tablespoon of broth or water, cover tightly, and cook until crisp-tender, about 8 minutes. Rinse and drain sauerkraut or salted cabbage. Heat in fat just to warm through.

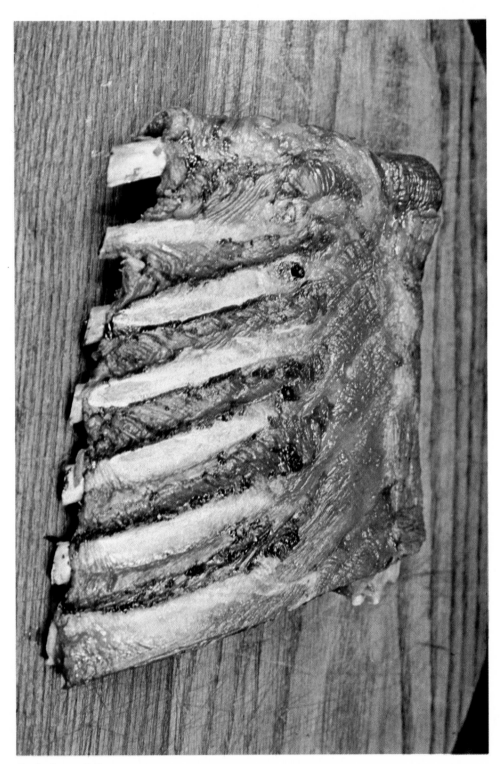

Basic Spare Ribs

BASIC SPARERIBS

1 pound spareribs for each person to be served

Heat the oven to 300° F. Wipe the ribs with a damp cloth and dry thoroughly. Cut into 4 or 5 ribs sections or leave in large pieces.

Place the ribs on a rack above a roasting pan. (It should be fairly deep since a lot of fat will cook out of the ribs.) Place the ribs in the oven and cook until very done and tender, about 1½ hours. They will be crusty and dark brown, and best of all, they couldn't be easier to make.

The ribs can also be roasted longer at 250° F, say about 3½ hours. This is a good way to cook them when you have to be away from home in the afternoon but must serve a memorable meal soon after getting back.

When the ribs are done, they are ready to receive any sauce you care to serve with them. Traditional accompaniments include:

hot Chinese mustard
duk sauce (Buy it in the supermarket, near the water chestnuts.)
plain soy sauce
equal parts soy sauce and sherry simmered with a few slices of
fresh ginger and 2 tablespoons chopped scallions

PIG'S FEET WITH HOT PEPPERS

1 recipe Basic Pig's Feet
1 7″ chili pasilla or 2 chilis serranos or other hot green peppers
1 red bell pepper cut in 1″ squares
1 green bell pepper cut in 1″ squares

Prepare the pig's feet according to the basic recipe. Fifteen minutes before the feet are tender, add the hot chilis and the bell peppers to the pot. Leave the dried chili pasilla whole; it will soften and release its flavor as the cooking liquid simmers. Seed and slice green hot peppers.

Serve the feet according to directions in the basic recipe. Retrieve the chili pasilla and put on the table as a condiment. Garnish feet with red and green bell pepper squares. Use some of the hot green chili slices if your diners are avid for hot food, otherwise discard.

BASIC BOILED BEEF

    3 to 4 pounds shin or shank of beef cut in large chunks or the same
      amount of rump or bottom round in one chunk
1 ½ cups water
    ½ cup soy sauce
    2 tablespoons sweet sherry
    3 scallions or 1 small onion, sliced
    1 piece of fresh ginger about 1″ × ½″, sliced

Put the meat in a heavy pot with a tight lid. Add the water and
bring it to a boil. Add the rest of the ingredients and bring to a
boil again. Now cover and reduce the heat so the liquid barely simmers. Cook very slowly until the meat is very, very tender, probably
3 or 4 hours.

If you have used shin or shank, the liquid will jell when it cools,
and any fat will be easy to remove. The meat is even better reheated
in the juice than it was the first time!

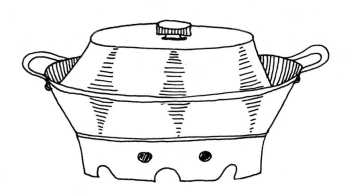

Beef with Watercress

BEEF WITH WATERCRESS

½ pound fillet of beef
½ of a large bunch of watercress, about 30 sprigs
2 or 3 chilis serranos
½ cup unsalted stock or water
1 tablespoon soy sauce
¼ teaspoon sugar
¼ teaspoon dry mustard
2 cloves garlic, minced
1 tablespoon oil

Remove all membrane and fat from the beef. Slice it very thin, then cut it into strips about 2″ × ½″. Wash and dry the watercress, remove the coarse stems (use them in soup), and roughly chop the leaves. Remove the seeds from the chilis and discard them; chop the chilis very fine.

Combine the stock, soy sauce, sugar, mustard, and garlic in a saucepan and bring to a boil. Reduce heat to simmering and cook about 5 minutes; the sauce will have reduced and thickened a little. In a heavy skillet heat the oil. Add the beef slices and cook quickly, stirring constantly. Only a minute or two will be needed; the beef needs only to lose its red color. Stir in the minced chilis and pour the sauce over the meat. Remove from the heat and stir in the watercress. Place in a covered serving dish and take to the table. By the time the dish is served, the watercress will be properly wilted but not ruined by too much heat.

STEAK WITH GINGER AND GARLIC

1 pound flank or round steak in one piece
2 cloves garlic, minced
1 tablespoon oil
1 teaspoon lemon juice
1 piece fresh ginger about 1″ × ½″, minced
1 tablespoon honey
1 medium onion, sliced
2 tablespoons lard

Wipe the steak with a damp cloth. Mix the rest of the ingredients except the lard and rub well into the steak. (Process the marinade in a blender until smooth if you have one.) Let stand at least 4 hours. (Overnight in the refrigerator would be even better.)

When ready to cook, cut the steak into very thin slices across the grain. Heat the lard in a heavy skillet and cook beef slices 3 minutes, stirring constantly. Remove to a serving plate and add 2 tablespoons soy sauce and 1 tablespoon dry sherry to the pan. Stir to collect any bits stuck to the pan and pour over sliced steak.

BEEF WITH ONIONS

½ **pound fillet of beef**
2 **large mild onions (or 10 scallions, green part and all)**
1 **teaspoon sugar**
2 **teaspoons sweet sherry**
2 **teaspoons soy sauce**
1 **teaspoon salt**
1 **tablespoon oil**

Remove all fat and membrane from the beef and cut it into very thin pieces 1½″ × ½″. Slice the onions thin, then cut each slice in half. Mix the rest of the ingredients except the oil with the beef and toss well.

Heat the oil in a skillet. Add the onions and cook for about 3 minutes; they should not brown at all. Remove the onions and set aside. Add the steak slices to the pan and cook very quickly, stirring constantly. (If the skillet is very dry, add a little more oil to cook the beef.) Return the onions to the pan and stir only to heat through. Serve at once.

This recipe is also good made with shredded beef: Cut each slice so that very thin matchsticks of beef are made. Fillet is easier to slice thin if it is very cold or slightly frozen.

Oxtail Stew

OXTAIL STEW

2 to 3 pounds oxtail cut in 1″ section (This is how it is usually packaged at the supermarket.)
1 quart water
½ cup soy sauce
¼ cup dry sherry
1 piece of fresh ginger about 2″ × ½″, sliced
2 cups vegetable of choice or combination of vegetables
1 cup diced celery

Wipe the oxtail pieces with a damp cloth to remove any bone dust that might be clinging to them where they were cut up—it isn't so tasty in the stew. Place the oxtail in a large heavy kettle with a tight lid. Add the water and bring to a rolling boil. Add the soy sauce, sherry, and fresh ginger (if fresh ginger is not available, use ½ teaspoon fresh ground ginger—not as good but better than none) and bring liquid to a boil again. Cover the pot and simmer until the oxtail meat is very tender and falls off the bone. Let the stew cool a little, then remove the bones. This is easier if you have a large slotted spoon or a colander through which to strain the broth. Discard the bones, or put them in another pot of soup; there won't be much taste left in them, but the texture they impart will be nice. Skim off all the fat you can, or better yet, put the broth and meat in the refrigerator overnight. Then the fat will be very easy to remove.

Reheat the stew; if you wish to add vegetables, cut in attractive chunks and simmer in stew for the time required to cook them tender. Add the celery the last 15 minutes for greenery and crunchiness.

BRAISED SHORTRIBS

1 pound of ribs for each person to be served
¼ cup soy sauce
¼ cup sweet sherry
1 medium onion, chopped roughly
1 piece of fresh ginger about 1″ × ½″, sliced

Wipe the ribs with a damp cloth. Place them in a heavy pan with a tight lid and add the other ingredients plus enough water or stock to make the liquid 1½″ deep in the pot. Bring the liquid to a boil and stir so that all ribs are coated. Cover the pan and reduce the heat to simmering. Cook over as low heat as is possible for 2 hours. Check the ribs for tenderness. If they are very tender, remove from the pan and drain well. Brown under the broiler for a few minutes on each side; do not let them burn.

Strain the braising liquid and remove all the fat you can from it. (There will be a lot.) Cook the defatted stock over high heat for a minute or two to reduce and thicken slightly. Serve with ribs.

A variation of this recipe is quite elegant:

BEEF IN JELLED BROTH

Follow the recipe for Braised Shortribs until ribs are tender, then let them cool in the cooking liquid. Remove them and take bones and fat off the meat; leave the meat in as large pieces as possible. Strain the braising liquid and let it cool. Remove all the fat and discard it.

Place the lean meat in a bowl or pan. Pour the defatted broth over the meat and put in the refrigerator until the broth sets, usually overnight. Unmold the jelled beef on a cold platter and garnish with watercress. Serve freshly grated horseradish and soy sauce to add to taste.

BEEF WITH ONIONS AND RED WINE

½ **pound round steak or roast**
10 **scallions**
 1 **teaspoon sugar**
 2 **tablespoons lard**
¼ **cup good dry red wine**
 1 **teaspoon soy sauce**
½ **teaspoon salt**

Remove all fat and membrane from the beef and cut it into very thin slices across the grain, as for London broil. Cut each slice into 2″ strips. Slice the scallions lengthwise, then diagonally in ½″ pieces. Sprinkle the meat with sugar and let stand 5 minutes.

Heat the lard in a skillet and quickly brown the steak on both sides. Add the wine, soy sauce, and salt to the pan and cover tightly. Reduce heat as low as possible and simmer for 3 minutes. Test meat. It should be tender. Cook a minute or two more if necessary. When meat is tender, add scallions and cook 1 more minute at high heat. Remove meat and scallions to a serving plate and continue cooking the liquid to reduce it and thicken it slightly. (Play it by ear here; sometimes the meat absorbs more, sometimes less.) Pour sauce over meat and serve at once.

Round steak is good meat for this dish since it has to simmer in the wine. Fillet would just get surly.

Ingredients for Pork Liver with Mushrooms and Scallions (page 106)

LIVER

Pork liver is inexpensive and delicious; it is rich in iron and other nutrients. Beef and lamb liver are also good buys—lamb liver has excellent supplies of vitamin A, while beef tops veal in vitamin A and has fewer calories per serving.

Liver of any kind should not be overcooked. To use it in any recipe for chicken livers or for sliced meat, have liver cut thin (about ¼″) by the butcher. If you buy packaged liver that is thicker, freeze it to make slicing easier. Or place the thick slice between two plates, the bottom one top down, the upper one top up, and slice the liver while pressing firmly on the top plate. Cut the thin slices into 1″ × 1″ pieces. Cut 1″ × ½″ pieces for recipes requiring shredded meat. Whatever the recipe, cook the liver only until it loses its red color. It will be done from the heat already present by the time the dish is served.

Recipes especially good with liver are: Sliced Pork with Sweet and Hot Peppers and Stuffed Hot Peppers

PORK LIVER WITH MUSHROOMS AND SCALLIONS

½ pound pork liver cut in thin 1½″ squares
10 dried black mushrooms or 10 large fresh mushrooms
10 scallions
 1 tablespoon oil
¼ cup dry vermouth
 2 tablespoons soy sauce
 1 teaspoon lemon juice

Dry the liver pieces with paper towels. Put dried mushrooms to soak in hot water for 5 minutes; cut fresh mushrooms into thick slices, stems and all. Slice the scallions in ½″ pieces. When dried mushrooms are reconstituted, slice them in ¼″ slivers.

Heat the oil in a heavy skillet. Cook fresh mushrooms 10 minutes over low heat, stirring often. Then add the liver and scallions and cook only until the liver loses its red color on both sides. If dried reconstituted mushrooms are used, add mushrooms, liver, and scallions at once and cook just until the liver loses its color.

While the meat and vegetables cook, mix vermouth and soy sauce. Pour into the pan and stir quickly to deglaze. Put the meat and vegetables on a serving plate and pour sauce from pan over it. Sprinkle with lemon juice. Pass the pepper grinder at the table.

THE
INSIDE
OF
THE
ANIMAL

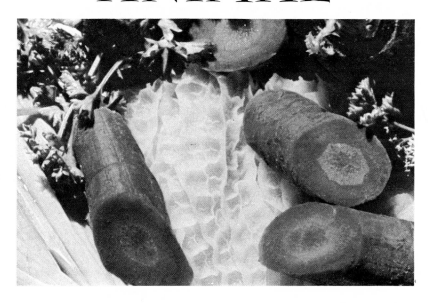

THE
INSIDE
OF
THE
ANIMAL

For centuries China has had a lot of people and no food to waste. Every part of the animal is used, and delicious recipes have been devised for cooking the organ meats. They are also very good for you, having a concentration of vitamins and minerals that the muscle meats (steaks, roasts) might envy. Do try them.

TRIPE

Tripe can be off-putting if you've never dealt with it. I take the liberty of stealing my own essay on the subject from another book and hope it will take the mystery out of tripe.

The thing about tripe is that it was once, and not so long ago, the outside part of an intestine. Whether it is from the pervasive influence of toilet training on the generation now wielding power in the kitchen or from some other, darker influence, the most common attitude toward tripe among otherwise good and sensitive cooks is, "Oh my God, NO!"

To be sure, careless slaughterhouses and butchers have a lot to answer for. When an animal is slaughtered, the man cutting the animal up has many chances to pierce the intestines and contaminate the outside portion with fecal matter. Such contamination need not be dangerous (boiling does wonderful things), but it is certainly not going to make a purchaser of the tripe in question dance and sing. And to be fair, it is often very difficult to extract the edible tripe in the best possible condition. But it can be done; indeed, it is done. Otherwise, half the Continental restaurants in metropolitan areas would have to shut down tomorrow. The question, then, boils down to getting good tripe and then knowing how to cook it. To get quality tripe, fix a custom butcher (there is nobody to blame at the supermarket if the worst happens) with a beady eye and tell him you want x pounds of y, z tripe. X: If you can freeze it, ask for 2 or 3 pounds; if you can't store it yourself, demand the quantity you really need. The larger amount is more impressive, but then you've *got* it. Y: This designates whether you want honeycomb, flat, or straight tripe. Honeycomb looks like it sounds: beeswax in the hive. Flat tripe comes in a sheet and is easier to work with. Straight tripe, usually sold only from lamb, looks like empty white sausage casings. Z is the animal from which you want the tripe. There is not much difference in the intrinsic qualities of different animals' tripe; mostly, the size of the animal determines the size of the tripe and that's about it. In general, ask for flat tripe (of whatever animal) and see what happens. Remember to look stern. Then you can deal with the butcher and settle for whatever he can supply—if it is of good quality. Place your order several days before you need the tripe; the butcher may not usually carry it and may have to buy it at the wholesale market. This is some trouble for you but a very good sign; at least you aren't getting last week's tripe!

Before getting on to the cooking, we must deal with what is good quality tripe. Whatever type and kind, it will be clean and white or whitish. It will smell something like a new shoe or a new book or a hot day in a tropical port, depending on your experiences and associations. What it will *not* smell like, if you want it, is intestinal waste. When you begin to cook it, there may be whiffs of odors you don't care for, but they shouldn't overcome you. Persevere through 2 or 3 changes of water. If there is no improvement, you can take the tripe back to the butcher and say that it doesn't meet your standards. Don't go into particulars; he can't argue with your flat statement. You may not get your money back (not much, since it is so cheap), but you will know to go to another store next time.

But on the point of good tripe, to summarize: As it cooks the first two or three times, it will *not* smell very good. Don't worry. If it smells foul, take it back.

Hang in there.

Proper cooking starts with thorough precooking. See the recipe for Basic Tripe. It works for other kinds as well. The meat should be fork-tender and the broth should be smelling like something edible, if a little like school glue.

Cooked tripe can be used in all recipes for sliced meat or shredded meats cut in the appropriate pieces and add to the cooking pan for just enough time to heat through. Slices of tripe may be sizzled in hot fat to brown on both sides before adding to other ingredients.

BASIC TRIPE

1 pound cleaned tripe
  water
  salt
  lemon slices

Rinse the tripe well in cold water. Put it in a heavy pan and cover with water. Add 1 teaspoon salt and one ¼″ slice of lemon. Bring the water to a boil and cook about 5 minutes.

Pour the water off, rinse the tripe, and start all over. Repeat this process until the tripe smells like meat (rather than something else!) cooking. Three or four changes of water are usually enough. When it smells acceptable (all this is assuming the tripe came from the butcher raw), cover the pot and simmer until the tripe is very tender; a fork should go through it easily. Drain and cool. It is now ready for most recipes. It usually takes a long morning or a whole day to get the tripe to this stage, so plan accordingly.

If you bought the tripe cooked, steamed, or whatever your part of the country calls it, bring it to a boil in some salted, lemoned

Lamb Tripe with Coriander

water, anyway. Their definition of cooked may not be yours. If any deficiencies appear, proceed as above.

Usually tripe will be needed cut in squares or in small matchsticks. If it seems hard to cut, consider that it (1) needs more cooking or (2) would benefit from being frozen solid. Freezing makes fancy cutting much easier, and a thorough chilling never hurt anything.

LAMB TRIPE WITH CORIANDER

Beef or pork tripe work fine in this recipe. Lamb is traditional.

½ **pound cooked tripe**
 1 **chili pasilla about 7″ long**
 1 **tablespoon lard or peanut oil (Lard is better.)**
¾ **cup unsalted chicken stock or water**
 1 **tablespoon soy sauce**
 1 **clove garlic, chopped fine**
½ **teaspoon sugar**
 6 **dried black mushrooms soaked for 10 minutes in hot water**
½ **cup chopped fresh coriander, stems and all**
 2 **or 3 whole sprigs fresh coriander for garnish**

Cut the tripe into fine slivers; it should look like matchsticks about 2½″ long. Dry well with paper towels.

Barely cover the chili with hot water and let it stand 10 minutes. Carefully cut it into ⅛″ slices. Remove the seeds and discard them—they are much too hot. Dry chili slices with paper towels.

In a heavy skillet heat the lard or oil until it is very hot. Toss the chili slices in the fat for a moment to coat; let them wilt, but do not let them burn. Reduce heat and add stock, soy sauce, garlic, and sugar; simmer about 10 minutes.

Drain the mushrooms and cut them in ⅛″ slices. Dry thoroughly. Add tripe shreds and mushrooms to sauce and stir to coat; cook just enough to heat through. Stir in chopped coriander and remove from heat at once. Transfer to a warm serving dish and garnish with sprigs of fresh coriander; serve at once. Flour pancakes are very good with this dish.

TRIPE SIMMERED WITH VEGETABLES

2 pounds raw tripe, parboiled
4 cups water
¼ cup soy sauce
½ cup sherry
2 whole scallions, sliced
2 cups vegetables

When the tripe has been parboiled until it smells good, put it in a big pot with the water and cook it, barely simmering, until it is tender, about 2 hours. Remove the tripe and cut it into 1″ squares. Return to the pot and add the soy sauce, sherry, and scallions. Cook another hour. The tripe stew can be served as it is, or vegetables can be added during the final hour of cooking. Cut the vegetables into attractive chunks and add so that they are just tender when the stew is done. For instance, add the carrots or turnips (or a combination of the two) at the beginning of the final hour. Sliced onions, peppers, shredded cabbage, broccoli, or cauliflower would go into the pot for the last 15 minutes.

STIR-FRIED VEAL HEART

1 ½ **pounds veal heart (If you have to buy the whole thing, extract 2 cups**
    of slices for this dish and put the rest in stew.)
  2 **tablespoons soy sauce**
  1 **tablespoon sugar**
  1 **small onion, diced**
  1 **teaspoon cornstarch**
  1 **piece of fresh ginger about 2″ × ½″, sliced**
  3 **tablespoons lard**

Ask the butcher to cut the heart lengthwise for you, then across
into ⅛″ slices. Or do it yourself. Clean off all blood vessels, blood
clots, and membranes. (This sounds worse than it is.) Mix the heart
slices with the rest of the ingredients except the lard and let stand
5 minutes.

Heat the lard in a heavy skillet. Add the beef mixture and stir
fry for 3 minutes. Serve hot at once. Raw spinach salad is very
good with this dish.

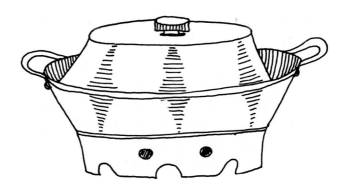

Ingredients for Tripe Simmered with Vegetables

SIMMERED AND FRIED BRAINS

    1 set calf's or beef brains
    ¼ cup unsalted chicken broth or water
    2 teaspoons soy sauce
    2 teaspoons sweet sherry
    1 tablespoon oil
    1 scallion, chopped, for garnish

Cut the brains into 1½" squares. Place in a heavy skillet with a lid and add the rest of the ingredients except the oil and scallions. Bring to a boil, then reduce heat and simmer covered for 10 minutes. Remove cover and turn the heat up to moderate. The brains should be set and firmer now. Watch the pan carefully. When the liquid is very low, add the oil. When the pan begins to sizzle, stir and fry the brains for 2 minutes. They should be lightly browned. Turn so that all sides of the pieces cook.

   Put on a warmed serving plate and garnish with the chopped scallion. Pass the soy sauce at the table.

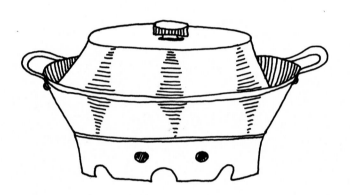

VEGETABLES

VEGETABLES

The variety of vegetables in China is endless. They are less often served alone than here—usually they are incorporated into dishes with meat as well. Chinese vegetables are not overcooked, which accounts for much of their attractiveness and nutritional value. Be sure to cook each vegetable just enough so that it is tender-crisp and still bright in color. And try not to boil vegetables; besides leeching out many of the vitamins and minerals, it is almost impossible to keep from overcooking. Use a steamer (a colander to hold the vegetables resting in a saucepan with a ½″ of water in it, not touching the vegetables, and a lid will steam small amounts) or stir fry vegetables in oil. If the vegetable you are preparing needs more cooking than stir frying provides, add a teaspoon or two of broth or water, cover the pan, and cook another minute or two. Be sure to drain off all the oil and cooking liquid before serving.

Sometimes one does wish to serve a plain cooked vegetable with a tasty but simple sauce. This recipe approximates a hot dressing often served in Hunan restaurants.

  1 tablespoon oil
  1 tablespoon butter (This is not authentic, but it tastes authentic.)
  ½ teaspoon dry mustard
  2 tablespoons soy sauce

Combine the ingredients and heat gently (perhaps over the pilot light) just long enough to melt the butter. Stir well. This sauce is particularly good on crisp steamed broccoli.

ROASTED SWEET POTATOES

Sweet potatoes are usually eaten as a snack in China, and they make a very good one, too.

1 medium-sized sweet potato per person

Wash and dry the sweet potatoes. Prick them well with a fork or sharp knife and place in a 325° F. oven for 1 hour or until tender. Let cool enough to eat or eat cold.

Sweet potatoes may be roasted on a *very* slow grill as well. In that case wash, dry, and prick them and wrap in two thicknesses of heavy-duty aluminum foil. Cook far away from the heat until the potatoes feel soft through the foil.

BRAISED EGGPLANT

1 medium eggplant
2 tablespoons lard
2 cloves garlic, minced
½ cup water
1 tablespoon soy sauce

Cut the eggplant in egg-sized chunks; do not peel. Heat the lard in a skillet with a lid and brown the eggplant pieces on all sides over moderate heat. Add the garlic, water, and soy sauce and cover the pan. Reduce heat and cook slowly for 10 minutes. Check for tenderness; the eggplant should be fork-tender but not falling apart.

Braised Eggplant (page 123)

BRAISED EGGPLANT WITH SHRIMP

1 recipe Braised Eggplant
1 cup raw or dried shrimp

Cook the eggplant according to the basic recipe through the browning process. Clean raw shrimp; soak dried shrimp in hot water until they are tender. Add raw shrimp to the skillet when the eggplant is checked for tenderness. They will be done in 1 or 2 minutes, depending on size. Add reconstituted dried shrimp for just long enough to heat through.

BRAISED RED CABBAGE

1 head red cabbage cut in ¼″ shreds
1 large onion, sliced
1 large apple cored but not pared, diced
1 tablespoon oil

Cut the cabbage, onion, and apple. Heat the oil in a heavy pot with a tight lid. Add the cabbage and stir well to coat with oil. Add the onion and cover the pan. Reduce the heat so that it is as low as possible. Cook about 5 minutes, then add the apple and stir well. Cook 3 minutes more and serve.

This cabbage is especially good with dry-marinated roast pork.

YELLOW AND GREEN SUMMER SQUASH

2 zucchinis
2 yellow summer squash
1 tablespoon oil
1 tablespoon grated onion
1 teaspoon soy sauce

Wash and dry the squash but do not peel them. Slice diagonally into 1″ chunks. Heat the oil in a heavy pan with a tight lid. Add the squash and stir well to coat all the pieces with oil. Cook over high heat long enough for steam to begin rising from the vegetables, then cover and reduce the heat as much as possible. Cook for 8 minutes, shaking the pan occasionally to prevent sticking. Check the squash. It should be beginning to be tender. Add the onion and soy sauce and cover again. Simmer until the squash is crisp-tender. Serve with coarse black pepper.

Braised Eggplant with Peppers and Onion

BRAISED EGGPLANT WITH PEPPERS AND ONION

 1 recipe Braised Eggplant (page 123)
 1 green bell pepper
 1 small hot green pepper
10 scallions or 1 large onion, sliced

Brown the eggplant according to basic recipe. Cut the bell pepper into 1″ squares. Seed the hot pepper and mince. When the liquid is added to the eggplant and the pan is covered, add the hot pepper. Add the bell pepper and onion slices when eggplant is tender; cook 2 more minutes, covered, with the heat increased to moderate. Serve at once.

BEANS WITH PORK

1 pound dried beans
2 pounds loin of pork, bone in
　　salt
　　sugar

Wash and look over the beans but do not soak them.

In a heavy pot with a tight lid brown the pork on all sides. Add the beans and enough water to cover them well. Add salt and sugar in the proportion of 1 teaspoon salt and ½ teaspoon sugar for each quart of water. Bring to a boil, then cover and reduce the heat so that the liquid barely simmers. Cook until the beans are tender, about 3 hours. Check the broth for seasonings; add more salt or soy sauce if necessary.

To serve, retrieve the pork and carve into thin slices. Put a slice of raw onion, then a slice of pork, into a soup bowl. Add beans and broth.

This dish is even better cooked the day before it is to be eaten and reheated. It keeps well in the refrigerator, too.

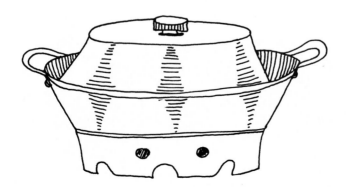

SALTED MUSTARD GREENS

2 pounds bright green mustard
2 tablespoons salt

Wash and pick over the mustard carefully. Dry with paper towels, then spread in the air to dry completely. Cut into 1½″ shreds and rub in the salt thoroughly.

Sterilize 4-pint glass canning jars and have two-piece lids on hand. Pack the mustard tightly into the jars (you may not need all 4—the greens compact a lot) so that there are no air spaces left. Seal and store in a cool place (not the refrigerator) for at least two weeks. It will turn yellow when it is ready to eat. Pour off the excess brine before using, or you may wish to rinse the greens in cold water for a milder flavor.

Vegetables for steeping

STEEPED VEGETABLES

one very large earthenware pot with a lid
firm vegetables in perfect condition: broccoli, cauliflower, green beans, bok
choy, white cabbage, red cabbage, sweet radishes, turnips, green and
yellow summer squash, red and green bell peppers, hot green peppers,
cucumbers, onions, whatever is in season
boiled water
salt

Wash the pot thoroughly with boiling water and let drain dry.

Trim the vegetables; leave whole if possible. (The kind of vegetable dictates whether to cut up or not: Broccoli and cauliflower should be broken into flowerets, not too small; bell peppers halved and the seeds and stems discarded; hot green peppers left whole, green beans whole, onions whole, etc.) Use boiled water if the vegetables need to be washed.

Arrange the vegetables in the pot. Put the largest ones on the bottom. Add boiled water, keeping track of how much is used, to cover the vegetables by 2 or 3 inches. Add 1 tablespoon salt for each cup of water. Seal up the pot with a paste made of flour and water and let stand for at least 2 weeks in a cool place. Add more vegetables as you use the ones in the pot.

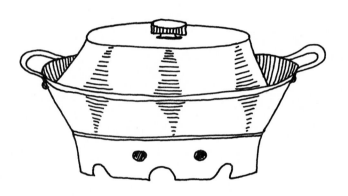

SOUPS

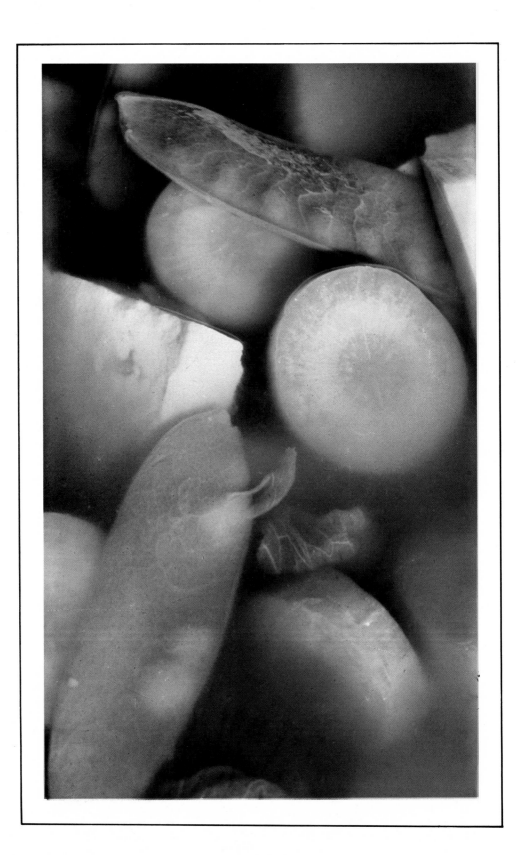

SOUPS

Soup is served throughout the two main meals in China. A bland soup
will cool down the spicy dishes; a perky one will pep up a mild
meal. Almost every kind of soup imaginable is eaten, and the variations are endless, from clear unsalted chicken broth to thick stews.
If soup is served first, Western style, it should be light enough not
to spoil appetites.

The most important element in any soup is the stock with which
it starts. Begin the stock several days before you plan to use it
so that it can cool and be defatted. Freeze stock not needed at
once; it keeps very well.

WHITE STOCK

4 **pounds chicken wings, necks, and backs (and some feet, if you can get them) or a stewing fowl**
1 **onion stuck with a whole clove**
2 **large carrots**
3 **or 4 stalks of celery, leaves and all**
1 **large parsnip**
½ **cup parsley**

Wash the chicken parts or the chicken. If you use a whole bird, tie it up so it will hold its shape; you will have the advantage of cooked chicken meat for many recipes. Cut the vegetables roughly. Put everything in a large pot and add 5 quarts water (or water to cover, depending on the pot.) Bring to a boil, then reduce the heat so that the liquid just simmers. Cook covered for 3 or 4 hours. Take out the chicken and strain stock. Let it get cold so fat will be easy to remove. Discard the vegetables used to make the stock (eat them yourself!), except possibly the carrots. If you save them, store in the refrigerator covered.

If you should have to defat the stock without waiting for it to get cold, pour it into a tall container, such as a milk bottle placed in the sink or a large pan; when the container if full, the fat will be at the top. Pour more stock in slowly so that the fat overflows and runs away. This is tedious and somewhat messy, but it is more effective than trying to skim a large container of stock.

BROWN STOCK

4 or 5 pounds of beef bones, including a knuckle, if possible
1 pound stewing beef, shin preferably
   vegetables from recipe for White Stock
½ cup soy sauce

Wipe the beef bones to remove any bone dust left when they were sawed up. Heat a large heavy pot and brown the bones and meat well; careful browning over medium heat goes a long way to make both the color and taste of this stock right. Add the vegetables, soy sauce, and 4 or 5 quarts of water. Cook 4 to 5 hours, simmering gently, covered. Discard bones when stock is done; strain and discard vegetables (eat those you like) and defat the stock when it has become cold.

See the recipe for White Stock for method of defatting while the soup is still warm.

Ingredients for Pork and Cabbage Soup

PORK AND CABBAGE SOUP

8 cups white stock, or make stock from pork bones alone or in combination with chicken
2 pounds lean boneless pork
1 small head red or white cabbage or bok choy
  soy sauce to taste

Heat the stock to boiling. In a skillet brown the meat, cut into 1½″ cubes, in a little lard. Put the pork in the stock and cook, barely simmering, until the pork is quite tender, about 1½ hours.

Shred the cabbage in ¼″ pieces and add to the soup. Continue to cook another 15 minutes or until the cabbage is quite tender but not disintegrating. Taste for seasoning and add soy sauce to taste.

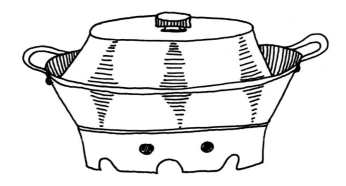

PORK AND WATERCRESS SOUP

Follow directions for Pork and Cabbage Soup except add 1 cup chopped watercress leaves and 1 tablespoon cornstarch mixed with a little cold water to the stock for the last 15 minutes of cooking time. Sprinkle with grated fresh ginger (about ¼ teaspoon for each serving).

BEEF AND BOK CHOY SOUP

Use dark stock instead of white and beef instead of pork in the recipe for Pork and Cabbage Soup. Cook until the beef chunks are tender, about 2 hours. Add bok choy for last 8 minutes.

BEEF SOUP WITH WATERCRESS

Use dark stock and beef in Pork and Cabbage Soup recipe. Add chopped watercress for the last 5 minutes of cooking time (no cornstarch in this version). Add ¼ cup dry sherry just before serving and taste for seasonings. Add soy sauce as needed. This is a very elegant soup indeed. You might want to cut the beef a little smaller (and neater) when making it.

CHICKEN BROTH WITH VEGETABLES AND HOT PEPPERS

6 cups chicken stock (or 1 cup for each diner)
1 chicken leg or thigh for each diner
1 cup whole tender green beans
1 small onion, minced
1 carrot sliced thin
1 dried chili pasilla for each diner

Bring the chicken broth to a boil and add the rest of the ingredients except the chili. Cover and reduce the heat so that the broth barely simmers. Cook until chicken is tender, about 15 minutes.

Serve in large bowls. Make sure everyone gets some of each vegetable. Lay the dried chili in the soup and serve. Each diner has as much or as little influence of the chili as he likes depending on whether he lets it steep in the soup (medium), breaks it up with his spoon and eats some of it (very hot!!!), or takes it out at once (cowardly).

Duck Soup

DUCK SOUP

Yes, there really is Duck Soup, and yes it is easy to make.

 1 **6-pound duck**
 2 **quarts water**
 ½ **pound cured ham in one chunk**
10 **dried black mushrooms**
 1 **scallion, whole**
 1 **tablespoon soy sauce**

Clean the duck; make sure the oil sack has been removed. Put the duck in a large pot and add the water. Bring it to a boil; skim often as the scum rises. Cook briskly for about 15 minutes. Then reduce the heat so that the broth just simmers and add the ham, mushrooms, the scallion, and soy sauce. Cover and cook very slowly until the duck is very tender and the meat begins to fall off the bones. Skim off all the fat you can.

Slice the ham thin and cut up the duck; serve each person some of each thing.

Many variations of this soup are possible. For instance, add 2 cups shredded cabbage during the last 30 minutes of cooking, or add bok choy the last 15 minutes.

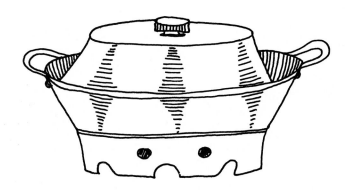

HOT POTS

HOT POTS

Big batches of impressive soup-stew, called pots, occupy an important place in Hunan cuisine, something like a cross between a standing rib roast and a spectacular chafing-dish effort in Western food. Some pots can indeed be cooked at the table (or a sideboard unless the table is huge), but others are prepared entirely in the kitchen and served from there in large soup plates. Don't worry about the protocol of the pot, however; just enjoy it.

You will need a very large cooking pot to cook the "pot" in. Earthenware or porcelain-clad iron work well. (The earthenware is lighter.) If the pot is beautiful, by all means bring it into the dining room and serve from it whether you have facilities for cooking it there or not.

Almost any ingredients can go into a pot. Let your imagination and available foods guide you. The recipes in this section make very good pots, but they are mainly suggestions instead of strict rules.

EVERYTHING-IN-A-POT

  4 **pounds pork shoulder or loin**
  1 **3-pound chicken, whole**
  1 **4-pound duck, whole**
  1 **cup soy sauce**
  ½ **cup sweet sherry**
  1 **piece fresh ginger about 2″ × ½″, sliced**
  2 **teaspoons salt**
 12 **hard .cooked eggs, shelled**
 20 **dried black mushrooms**
  1 **tablespoon sugar or honey**

This will require a really big pot, preferably one that is wide and shallow rather than narrow and deep.

Wipe the pork with a damp cloth and place in the pot. Add 4 cups water. Bring to a boil, then simmer, covered for 1 hour. Meanwhile wash the chicken and duck and tie them so they will hold their shape during cooking. Add them to the pot along with 1½ cups water, the soy sauce, sherry, ginger, and salt. Bring to a boil, then cover and simmer for 30 minutes. Now add the eggs, mushrooms, and sugar. Cover and simmer until the meat is very tender. To serve, slice the pork and cut the birds into serving pieces. Arrange the eggs around the edge of the (large) serving dish and scatter mushrooms over the meats. Give each diner some of everything, including the broth, in a large soup plate.

HUNAN POT I

Make a batch of brown stock according to the recipe in the section on soups. Add to it as it cooks:

2 turnips, scrubbed and roughly diced
2 more carrots
  the core from a head of white cabbage, cut in chunks
6 cloves of garlic (Don't worry about this much garlic; it gets
  amalgamated somehow.)

Simmer the stock very slowly for a long time, even overnight. Strain and defat the stock. You should have at least 3 quarts. Retrieve the carrots and stew meat and use when the pot is made. Discard bones and everything else.

To make the actual pot, return the stock to your big beautiful pot (it will jell if it gets cold) and bring it to a boil. Add to it:

1 more pound boneless stew meat cut in 1½″ cubes
2 new turnips, scrubbed and sliced ¼″ thick
1 new carrot, scrubbed and sliced ¼″ thick diagonally

Cook for 1 to 1½ hours, until the meat is very tender. Then add a selection of fresh green vegetables such as:

2 zucchinis, cut diagonally
2 yellow summer squash, cut diagonally
½ head white cabbage roughly shredded
1 cup broccoli flowerets
1 cup diced celery

Simmer the pot just long enough to cook the vegetables tender, about 15 minutes. Return carrots and meat from the broth preparation to the pot and cook enough longer to heat them through. Add salt

Hunan Pot I

or soy sauce to taste.

Serve the pot or let guests serve themselves. Try to make sure that everybody gets some of everything.

Any other vegetables are redundant with this pot. Plan a fruit dessert or make rice pudding.

HUNAN POT II

Make white stock according to the recipe in the section on soups.

To assemble the pot, bring the stock to a boil in your best-looking large cooking pot. Add to it a selection of light-colored, tender vegetables such as:

1 cup cauliflower flowerets
2 zucchinis, sliced diagonally
2 yellow summer squash, sliced diagonally
1 cup sliced scallions
1 cup snow peas
1 cup sliced white mushrooms
2 or more small white carrots or sweet radishes, sliced
2 turnips, peeled, sliced and cut in fancy shapes

Cook slowly until the vegetables are almost tender, about 15 minutes. Then add:

2 boned chicken breasts cut in 2″ squares
1 pound cleaned raw shrimp or reconstituted dried shrimp

Continue cooking just until the chicken and shrimp are white through, about 10 minutes at very low heat. Add salt to taste. As you see, considering what an impressive dish this is, it doesn't take long if the stock is made ahead. A raw spinach salad would be a handsome accompaniment for this white (well, light) pot.

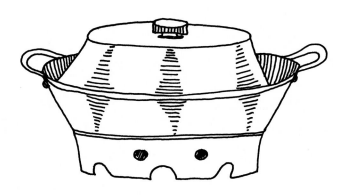

STARCHES

STARCHES

Rice in China is eaten with chopsticks, so a stickier texture is needed. If you have prided yourself on your rice's separate, fluffy grains, you will need to learn a new method to make nice gluey rice.

RICE

3 cups water
1 cup white rice

Bring the water to a boil and slowly stir in the rice. Cover the pan with a tight lid and reduce the heat as much as possible. Cook without stirring for about 40 minutes, or until all the water is

FLOUR PANCAKES

These thin flour crepes are very good, especially with hot and spicy meat dishes of Hunan and with Moo Shu Pork.

2 cups flour
1 cup boiling water
   oil

Sift the flour and add the water, which has been allowed just to stop boiling. Stir to make a dough and wrap it in foil or waxed paper when it cools slightly. Chill for an hour for easier handling.

When ready to cook, divide the dough into 16 balls. Place a piece of waxed paper on a smooth surface and brush it with oil. Pat a piece of dough into a flattened ball and place it on the paper. Brush the top of the dough with oil. Flatten another ball of dough and place it on top of the first one. Brush with oil and top with another sheet of waxed paper. Roll out to make 2 crepes about 5 or 6 inches in diameter. Repeat until all the dough is used up. To cook, heat a skillet or griddle over medium heat. Carefully separate the crepes and cook them one at a time for about 3 minutes on each side. They should not brown but only dry out somewhat. If they are to be eaten at once, place in a napkin-lined covered dish to keep hot. If you are cooking them ahead of time, wrap in foil and reheat on the griddle or in a slow oven when ready to eat.

QUICK SPRING ROLLS

These are quick because flour pancakes are used for the wrapping.

½ **pound shredded pork or chopped shrimp or a combination of the two**
1 **scallion, finely chopped**
½ **cup fresh pea sprouts or canned bean sprouts**
1 **tablespoon soy sauce**
1 **generous tablespoon lard**
16 **uncooked flour pancakes**
   oil for frying

Mix the first four ingredients and toss to mix well. Heat the lard in a heavy pan and add the meat-vegetable mixture. Stir and cook for 3 minutes, then remove from the heat and let cool a little.

Lay a pancake flat and put a tablespoon of the filling just to one side of the diameter. Spread it slightly so it lies in a rectangle parallel to the diameter. Now fold the ends of the pancake perpendicular to the filling in, then fold the side of the circle nearest the filling over it and finish by rolling the folded part over the unused semicircle. If that flap shows signs of not sealing well, brush with a little beaten egg yolk.

This sounds more complicated than it really is. The main thing is to get the filling enclosed in the pastry somehow so it won't leak.

Heat enough oil to make ¼″ in the skillet. Fry the spring rolls until they are golden on each side. Do not crowd them. To serve at once, slash each roll into 3 pieces diagonally and serve hot. Pass the soy sauce. If you are cooking ahead, drain the rolls, then reheat them in a 300° F. oven for 10 minutes before cutting and serving.

N.B. These are familiar appetizers, of course. Be sure to have plenty of napkins around if they are to be eaten with the fingers (perfectly proper, but greasy). Vary the filling according to your own ideas; almost any combination is good.

a

b

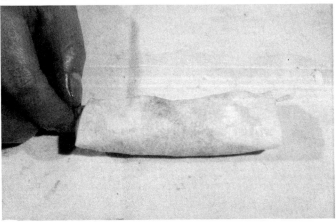

c

a) Place filling on dough. b) Fold back half of dough over filling and fold ends toward each other. c) Roll forward to seal front flap.

Quick Spring Rolls (page 159)

DESSERTS

DESSERTS

Desserts as such are not eaten as much in China as here. Fruit or rice pudding is enjoyed, but often as between-meal snacks. Whenever you have them, Chinese sweets are different and delicious—for instance, try the sweet bean paste!

SWEET BEAN PASTE

2 cups pinto beans
honey to taste

Wash and look over the beans. Cook them until they are very tender in water to cover generously. When they are done, process in the blender with just enough broth to keep the mixture from becoming solid—it should be quite stiff. Add enough honey to make a very sweet paste, about 3 tablespoons for each cup of bean paste. Store tightly covered in the refrigerator. It will keep for a week or two.

EIGHT-JEWEL RICE PUDDING

 1 pound short grain white rice
 3 cups water
 ½ cup sugar
 ¼ pound attractive candied fruit pieces

Cook the rice in 2 cups of water in a large heavy pan. Bring to a boil, then simmer about 30 minutes; the rice grains should be transparent around the edges but still opaque in the center. Add the other cup of water and the sugar. Bring to a boil, then reduce heat and simmer 15 minutes more, or until the rice is tender.

Grease a large heatproof bowl with solid vegetable shortening or butter (not authentic, but helpful later). Arrange the candied fruit in an attractive design in the bottom of the bowl. Spoon the rice mixture carefully into the bowl—don't displace the design. Put the bowl on a rack in a covered steamer and steam for about 3 hours; the rice should be *very* tender and the pudding firm.

Remove the cooked pudding from the steamer. Run a knife blade around the edge of the dish to loosen pudding. Put a serving dish over the steamer, then invert the steamer and platter to unmold the pudding. A smart tap on the bottom of the steamer may help it come out. (This is where the greasing of the steaming dish helps!)

Serve the pudding hot. If there are leftovers, store in the refrigerator but reheat before serving again. This dish is always served hot.

SAUTÉED BANANAS WITH SWEET BEAN PASTE

1 barely ripe banana for each person to be served
2 tablespoons sweet red bean paste for each banana
2 eggs, beaten
   flour
   oil for sautéing

Split the bananas lengthwise. Form 2 tablespoons of sweet bean paste into a long rope and place on one half of the banana. Then replace the other half of the banana and press down gently. Keep in the refrigerator until ready to cook.

Just before serving, cut the bananas into 1½″ chunks. Dip each one into the beaten eggs, then into the flour; sauté gently in oil ½″ deep over moderate heat. Turn to brown lightly on all sides. Handle banana pieces gently. Serve at once.

Sautéed Bananas with Sweet Bean Paste

SWEET-BEAN-PASTE PASTRIES

½ recipe flour pancake dough
   sweet red bean paste (See recipe above.)

Roll out the pancake dough to make very small circles, 3 or 4 inches in diameter. Place a spoonful of the bean paste on one side of the raw pancake and fold the other side over it. Press the edges together to seal. Fry in ¼″ oil in a skillet, turning to brown both sides and draining on paper towels. Or brush with oil and place on an oiled baking sheet and bake until golden in a 425° F. oven.

STUFFED PRUNES

1 pound prunes
1 cup almonds (optional—see directions)

If the prunes are soft and tender, slit each one carefully and remove the seed. If they are dry and hard, cover with boiling water and let stand 15 minutes. Then drain and dry; slit and remove seeds.

If you like the almondlike center of the prune seeds, carefully crack each prune seed and extract the tiny nut. Put it back inside a prune and press the edges of the slit to seal. Pack stuffed prunes into a dish with a cover, barely cover with cold water and store in the refrigerator until serving time. If you do not like the slightly bitter prune nut, use unblanched almonds to stuff the prunes; proceed as above. If you like both almonds and prune nuts, by all means use them both!

A sliver of candied orange peel or candied pineapple makes good stuffed prunes, too.

SQUASH IN SYRUP

winter squash—Hubbard, butternut, acorn—or pumpkin
syrup made in the proportion of 3 parts water, 4 parts sugar,
  1 part dark corn syrup

Choose firm unblemished squash. Wash and cut small ones in half; remove seeds and fibers and leave halves whole. Wash and halve larger squash and pumpkins, discard seeds and fibers, and cut in 3" × 4" pieces.

Place the squash in a large shallow pan and cover with water. Remove the squash and measure the water. Add sugar and corn syrup in the proportions given above. Bring syrup to a boil, then reduce heat so that it just simmers. Add the squash and cook very slowly (at the lowest heat possible) until the squash is very tender and the syrup is almost absorbed, about 1 hour. Very carefully remove pieces of squash to a glass serving dish and pour the remaining syrup over them. Serve at room temperature. Store leftovers in the refrigerator, covered, but reheat to melt the syrup before serving again. About 10 minutes in a 300° F. oven should do it.

BANANAS IN HONEY

   1 cup honey
  ½ cup sugar
  ½ cup water
   1 teaspoon cider vinegar
   1 or 2 barely ripe bananas for each diner
     a large shallow bowl of water with ice cubes (A soufflé dish would be
     good.)

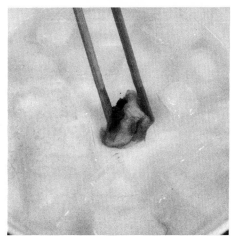

Combine honey, sugar, water, and vinegar in a saucepan. Cook until the syrup reaches 275° F. on a candy thermometer (soft-crack stage). Meanwhile, cut the bananas into 1″ chunks and place them on a serving plate. Prepare the ice water.

When the syrup is done, pour it over the banana chunks. Turn each piece to coat evenly (chopsticks are the best implements for this process) but handle gently. Take bananas and ice water to the table. Let guests take pieces of banana with their chopsticks, dip them into the ice water, then transfer them to their own plates to eat. The cold water hardens the syrup and makes the sugary shells around the fruit crisp.

Pared and cubed pears or apples can also be served this way. Sprinkle apple chunks with lemon juice to prevent their turning brown; omit vinegar from syrup.

HELPFUL
HINTS

HELPFUL HINTS

Bean curd: Canned bean curd is available from both Trinacria and Moneo's in New York City (see Sources for details). It is very good in almost all stir-fry recipes, and it adds the nutritional value of that super food, soybeans, to any dish it's used in. Add the curd cut in 1″ x 1″ x ½″ pieces and allow to just heat through in the sauce as the dish finishes cooking.

Freezing: A freezer is a great convenience for cooking Chinese food. It is especially useful for keeping stocks on hand; then delicious and otherwise quite time consuming dishes such as soups and pots can be made often. You can also save time by cooking large amounts of slow cooked meat at one time, using part one time and freezing the rest for another meal. Meats simmered in flavored sauces often actually improve in flavor and tenderness after freezing. This is assuming, of course, that the cooked meat has been quickly cooled, properly packaged, and frozen and stored at very cold temperatures.
Vegetables, on the other hand, do not come through the freezing process unscathed: the blanching process they are put through before freezing and the freezing and defrosting itself take the crisp bloom and bright color from most vegetables. An exception is tiny carrots that are often available only frozen or canned. The frozen ones are much better. In general, though, use your freezer to save time and effort in the meat and sauce parts of your dish and cook the vegetables from scratch.

Garlic: Garlic is such an important ingredient in Hunan food that it deserves additional comment. It is often thought that garlic lasts forever and that no special care need be taken in its purchase, storage, or use. This is not true. Garlic can get stale, and then it is quite awful. Buy only heads that are firm and tightly bunched. Slough off any dry thin membranes when you get it home, but do *not* wash it. Store in a tightly closed small glass jar in the refrigerator and use it up as fast as possible. If there is any doubt about your supply, peel a clove and look at it; if it is beginning to dry and darken, discard it. A small piece can effectively ruin a whole dish. You may find it useful to keep freeze-dried garlic bits on hand for emergencies. They are not quite as good as fresh garlic, but they are a lot better than garlic that is past its prime.

Monosodium glutamate: Sold under the retail name of Accent, this chemical flavor-enhancer is used with too heavy a hand by many restaurants, especially Chinese restaurants. (Remember the Chinese-Restaurant Syndrome? Some people get unpleasant physical side effects from the sudden intake of lots of MSG.) Besides, sprinkling MSG with a heavy hand makes everything taste alike after a while. A judicious pinch can revive flagging vegetables, but do use it sparingly. In general, Hunan food has so much flavor that it needs MSG the way Venice needs more canals.

Steamer: See Wok.

Substitutes: Most cooks substitute some ingredients for others at some times. You can certainly do the same in these recipes. If you have found successful changeabouts in other types of cooking, they will probably work in the recipes in this book, too. Don't be intimidated! Here are a few trial-and-error notes:

> **Dry whole ginger** can be substituted in many recipes for fresh ginger root. Use about half the volume of dry ginger as you would fresh. Smash it with a mallet to release the flavor. Retrieve the dry ginger before serving the dish; it is *not* edible the way fresh root is.

> **Ground dry ginger** is a useful spice in itself, but in most cases it will *not* substitute successfully for fresh. You will want to keep it on hand, however, because it is very good for "freshening" the taste of many other dishes. As for garlic, buy the smallest bulb possible, make sure the container is airtight, and store it in the refrigerator.

> **Chicken fat,** rendered, can usually be substituted for lard. *Lard* can usually be substituted for oil (unless the recipe specifically says not

to) except for deep frying. It is *possible* to deep fry in lard, but why incur the mess and the expense?

Onions and chives in combination can be substituted for scallions. (You don't want to substitute the whole amount of chives alone— the dish would be very hot and strange!) Use one medium onion for about each six scallions called for; add enough snipped chives to give a nice color and fresh taste.

Sweet vermouth is an acceptable substitute for sweet sherry in most dishes. Dry vermouth will fill in for dry sherry in an extreme emergency; however, it is a good and unusual replacement in any dish calling for a dry white wine.

Tea: Please do use moderation in serving tea with the dishes in this book. Tea throughout the meal will simply dilute the tastes. A hot beverage tends to cut the appetite (good for you if you're on a diet, but not the effect you want to produce on your dinner guests) and it will not be as effective a foil for spicy food as cold beer or chilled not-too-dry white wine. Or simply cold water.

Vitamin E: A 200-unit capsule of Vitamin E added to the oil for deep frying will keep it sweet and pure through several uses and will also prevent food from absorbing the unpleasant tastes of rancid oil. Simply pierce the capsule and squeeze the contents into the oil before it is heated the first time. Also, be sure to use a thermometer so that the oil will be used at the proper heat. Too high temperatures will lead to unpleasant smoking and unevenly cooked food.

Vitamin E is the very best first aid for kitchen burns, too. First let cold water run over the burn for several minutes. Then dry it off and squeeze the contents of a capsule directly onto the burn. This really works.

Wok: When you buy a new wok, it will need to be seasoned as an iron skillet does before you cook in it. If instructions come with your wok, follow them. Otherwise, wash, rinse and dry the wok well. Brush it with fresh unsalted fat and heat until very hot but not smoking. Reduce the heat as much as possible and let the wok stay hot for at least 30 minutes. Wipe out any excess oil standing on the surface and let the wok cool. Repeat once or twice more. If you burn the fat while seasoning, or if you later really burn on a bad stain, wash the pan then scour thoroughly with steel wool. Wash, dry and start the seasoning process all over again. If you have inadvertently used stale fat in the seasoning, do the scouring bit and then sniff; if an unpleasant odor remains, let the wok soak in a solution of 1 tablespoon baking soda to 2 quarts water for about 12 hours, then do the scouring and seasoning over again. This is a great bother; try to get really fresh fat the first time.

Some experts say you should never wash a seasoned wok, just as they advise against washing omelet pans. The time will almost certainly come when your wok needs washing thoroughly. Do it. A well-seasoned wok should come through a bath just fine. Just don't use steel wool or abrasive scouring powder.

An excellent *steamer* can be made from a wok with the addition of a flat perforated metal disk made to fit about one-third of the way up from the bottom of the wok. Tell the dealer the size of your wok and he can order it for you if you didn't get the rack when you bought your wok in the first place. Quite a large amount of food can be steamed in even a moderate-sized wok, and the shape of the pan has the advantage that if extra liquid is needed during steaming, it can be added by pouring it down the side of the wok without danger of splashing the steaming food.

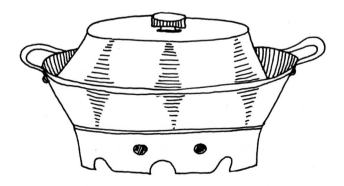

SOURCES

Two of the best sources of ingredients for Hunan cooking are not Chinese at all, but they have a good selection of hard-to-find groceries and are fast and reliable about filling mail orders.

Trinacria Importing Company, 415 Third Avenue, New York, New York 10016. This marvelous store carries a very full selection of ingredients for Chinese dishes, including fresh and dried (mailable) coriander, fresh ginger, canned bamboo shoots, bean curd, dried chestnuts, dried mushrooms, dried shrimp, and dried and canned hot peppers. Trinacria also sells large cans of some vegetables and fruits, convenient and economical when serving a large group.

To order, write your requests and send with your name, address (be sure to include the zip code since parcel post charges are calculated from zip codes), and a check or money order for the estimated cost of the order (no C.O.D.s). Trinacria will send you what they have that is mailable and within the deposit you sent. At this time there is no catalog, but letters of inquiry will be answered if you enclose a stamped self-addressed envelope. You will be amazed at the variety of Trinacria's stock; if you want it, they probably have it. If you are in New York, by all means go by and have one of their legendary hero sandwiches (to take out) and meet the wonderful people who run the store. Also, look over the selection of cheeses; you are sure to leave loaded down!

Casa Moneo Spanish Imports, 210 West 14th Street, New York, New York 10011. This store specializes in foods and all kinds of merchandise from Mexico and other Latin countries. They will fill mail orders for chilis (dried and canned), spices, cookware, and anything else mailable that they have in stock C.O.D. (minimum order $5.00, including postage) and send a catalog at the same time. Be sure to include your name, address, and zip code. If you are in New York, go by to look at the vast selection of sausages and cheeses, Spanish confections, exotic canned goods, clothes, jewelry, and the latest Latin records.

Cooking and eating Hunan food is a great adventure, one of those experiences that is just as good in actuality as it is in anticipation. I hope you will enjoy the recipes in this book as much as I've enjoyed researching and testing them. Writing the book was genuinely fun, and I like to think that is a good sign. Enjoy yourself!

INDEX

INDEX

Roasted Peking duck.

1. long Island duckling (about 4 lbs)
6 cups water
1/4 cup syrup or honey
1 stalk green onion
1 slice (thin) ginger

Wash and pat dry a whole long Island duckling. Boil duckling in a kettle (or large pan) with water, honey onion and ginger for 2 minutes (each side). Air dry duckling over night (minimum 24 hrs.). Two hours before dinner, bake duckling on rack in oven at 350° for 1 hr. Turn the oven down to 300° and turn duckling over and bake for 1/2 hr. Turn the oven back up to 375° and turn duckling again and bake for 20 minutes.

Slice duckling into thin slices and serve with pancake, hoisin sauce and raw green onions (sliced 2 inches long).

Pancake

1 1/2 cup water
3 cups flour (all purpose)
sesame oil.

Put flour in a mixing bowl. Bring water to a boil and pour into the flour gradually and stirring with spoon until blended. Let cook a little. Knead the mixture on a floured board until smooth (about 10 or 15 minutes) Cover dough with a damp cloth and let stand for 10 minutes. Form the dough into a long

roll about 2 inches in diameter. Cut roll in 1/2 inch
thick slices, and flatten to about 1/4 inch in
thickness. Brush one side of a round with sesame
oil. Place one unoiled round on top of the oiled
side of the first. Dust each pair with flour lightly
and roll out into a very thin pancake. Heat an
ungreased skillet over low heat and bake 1 pancake
at a time for about 2 minutes on each side or until
lightly colored. Transfer to a platter. Separate the
two halves and keep warm in steamer until all
pancakes are done. This recipe make 10 - 15 pancakes
depending on their thickness.

* boil water - to steam   Granger
  cold "   - to boil.